ETERNAL GOLD

ETERNAL GOLD

Third book of
THE TRILOGY OF TRUTH

as revealed to
Jean K. Foster

Request for such permission should be addressed to:

>Uni★Sun
>P.O. Box 25421
>Kansas City, MO 64119

This book is manufactured in the United States of America. Cover art by Darlene Merriott and distribution by The Talman Company:

>The Talman Company, Inc.
>150 Fifth Avenue
>New York, N. Y. 10011

ISBN # 0–912949–16–3
LCCN : 87–051687

Uni★Sun
BOOK

PROMISE TO THE READER

To those of you who read this book, or any book of *The Trilogy of Truth,* the Brotherhood of God promises to be with you as teacher and counselor. "We promise each reader that you will not read without our gentle presence, without our teamwork, without our enlightenment.

"In the earth plane there is much that wets (throws cold water on) truth, but these books enter the marketplace with the shining light of God within and without. They fairly leap into the arms of those who search the shelves to find grist for their searching minds."

Your Counselors, Your Comforters,
Your Teammates in the Search

Books by Jean K. Foster:

The God-Mind Connection	Spring 1987
The Truth That Goes Unclaimed	Fall 1987
Eternal Gold	Spring 1988

The above three volumes constitute "The Trilogy of Truth." In preparation are:

Epilogue	Fall 1988
The Truth That Must Be Told	Spring 1989

ETERNAL GOLD

God truth is the *eternal gold* that anyone can use to
create a wonderful lifetime experience.

When you make your God truth permanent within your
being, you are ready to make use of your *eternal gold.*

Teamwork is you working with the Brotherhood of God
through God-mind, and it is the way to use *eternal gold* in
all its creative potential.

When truth is a permanent part of your mind/spirit, the
law says you must demonstrate it into the earth plane.

The Brother of Brothers, the one people call Jesus of
Nazareth, talks to the reader about his lifetime on earth.

Team up with *wholeness,* not the parts which ache, hurt,
get tender, or which withdraw their participation in the
whole body.

Never think you should follow any plan another person
presents for you, nor should earth-mind truth influence

your decisions. Only God-mind can bring you the best truth for your assimilation.

Oneness with God, your Teammate, is what you must recognize, eternalize and understand if you are to make full use of *eternal gold.*

Pure Thought is your working material, according to the Brotherhood, and you must think of it as *matter*—not a vague, unsubstantial breeze that passes through your mind.

Mastering principles and a willingness to practice the demonstration procedure can lead you to successful results.

What God IS, what He wants of you, and what you might want of Him are the areas covered here.

A process is given by which you can give yourself to all that is God.

The Brother of Brothers, Jesus, describes what happens when God and you become true partners.

Gentle presences, part of the Brotherhood, help people reach their goals and their desires, but the one who must initiate action is you.

FOREWORD

To put "Eternal Gold" in its proper context, readers should know that this is the third in a series of channeled truth books written by Jean K. Foster. Through her own God-mind connection, she has been charged with the mission of explaining, informing and demonstrating how God-mind truth can enrich our lives on earth and enable each of us to attain our individual spiritual goals. She has been guided in this project by the Brotherhood of God, a group of advanced spirits on another plane.

As Jean's husband of 38 years, I have noted some rather obvious changes in her life style since she became a writer of channeled truth books. I am impressed with the development of her writing skills, her gift if you will, and her ease and speed in communicating with the Brotherhood and with God-mind. Even more significant, though, is her spiritual growth which is making quite an impact on our lives.

Jean first became aware of her mission in late 1984 following her request for a spiritual counselor to help her in her daily living. She has not only received much counseling since that time, but she was told by her counselor that she was to "write a tome." "The God-Mind Connection," published in Spring 1987, is a direct result of her spiritual counseling. This first book reveals the existence of the Brotherhood of God who are inspired by Jesus, the Brother of Brothers. The book explains that the Brotherhood exists to help those of us in the earth plane to connect with God-mind. As we demonstrate the perfect truth we receive from God-mind in our daily living, our planet earth benefits, and so do we.

When Jean finished "The God-Mind Connection," I assumed that was it. She had said it all in one volume. Obviously the Brotherhood didn't think so because in no time at all, a steady stream of spiritual guidance came to her. The channel to the Brotherhood, and ultimately to God-mind, was wide open.

The result was a second book, "The Truth that Goes Unclaimed," published in Fall 1987. This book points out that there is much truth—eternal and personal—that we can make use of, but we are not really aware of it. We may be aware of it in a subconscious way, but not in a conscious way. We are told to reach out and take hold of these truth principles that the Brotherhood tells us about, and apply them directly in our lives.

I knew better than to ask if there was to be a third book, since she was already receiving new material. This eventually developed into "Eternal Gold." What I didn't realize was that this first series of books was only the beginning, that there was to be a second trilogy to follow! However, I am getting ahead of myself, and I am only writing the foreword. How my wife manages to keep all of this communication straight—and organized into books—is beyond my comprehension.

"Eternal Gold," as do the first two books in the series, moves the reader forward into new concepts, new thoughts and specific ways to make use of God-mind truth. The books are, in effect, a step-by-step revelation of how each individual can deal directly with God, and even more important, apply God-mind truth to everyday living. In "The God-Mind Connection" and "The Truth that Goes Unclaimed," we are told that our perfect truth is out there and that we can claim it for our very own. In this third book, we find that the same truth can be the eternal gold that we can use to enhance our lives in every respect. "Eternal Gold" specifically relates to such things as bodily wholeness, prosperity, successfully meeting our personal problems and teamwork with the God of the Universe.

Long before "Eternal Gold" was sent to the publisher for typesetting, Jean was receiving channeled material for a second trilogy which, according to her sources, is destined to become a textbook for the New Age. It, too, is in three parts.

The first part deals with why the New Age must come about and how we will benefit from it. Through creative cooperation with God we can survive, and we can also help others to survive and live well. A rough draft of this book is completed.

The next book deals with learning how to become a master of greatness. That may well become its title, since the book deals with those readers who want to become candidates for a Master of Greatness. By mastering the use of eternal and personal truth, the necessities and the desires of life can be readily obtained. As of this writing, Jean doesn't have any idea what the third book in this second trilogy will cover, but I know that when it comes to her, it will be even more enlightening and useful than the others.

Somewhere in between and during the writing of the first and second trilogies, Jean developed a wide range of contacts with spirits who recently left earth, and she has compiled these stories in book form and titled it "Epilogue." Included are stories from the spirits of those who are now in a second plane of life. These stories relate to the life they lived on earth and what they have found in the next plane along with the perspective they have about it all. To say that it is fascinating reading is the understatement of the year. We don't know just when "Epilogue" will be published, but hope it will be in the fall of 1988. She is also collaborating with an artist friend, working on an illustrated truth book for pre-school children.

I mentioned earlier that Jean has undergone some dramatic changes in her spiritual life. In a sense she has said goodbye to her old way of life as a church leader, Sunday school teacher and vacation Bible school teacher. As she once put it, "If the church doors were open, I was there. Almost all the time." She has always had spiritual goals, but in the past, she found the answers to her questions within the structure of the church. She was very orthodox in her beliefs and leaned heavily on the Bible for explanation and authority, although you could never call her a fundamentalist or Bible literalist. Sometimes she would put pressure on me to squeeze through the same knothole she then believed to be the way to salvation.

But, through the years her attitudes changed, and since she started writing channeled books, these changes have been much more obvious. We still attend church, but she is no longer a member. I think it is because she feels restricted by the vows of membership and some of the church dogma which she no longer accepts.

Unfortunately, a few of Jean's former close friends have closed their minds to her books. But, she is discovering new friends whose minds are open, and they and she enjoy a rich sharing of spiritual growth.

We recently took communion in church and while most of us took the bread and wine in remembrance of Jesus dying on the cross, Jean received a meditation, "Do this in remembrance of Jesus' understanding of Truth." It is a new way of life in which she depends on her God-mind connection for her stable Source of Truth. She keeps a notebook which she calls her "Record of My God-mind Connection," and it is filled with personal, private records. She does not share these with me, since they are her own personal truths.

We will never go back to our old way of life. My wife is happier, filled with enthusiasm, and much more adventurous and willing to "entrepreneur" new projects or ideas. The former traditional, conservative, reluctant-to-splurge-on-the-nicer-things-in-life Jean exists no longer. I know it is a change for the better. The other day I backed our brand new station wagon out of the garage and accidentally left the rear door open. It made a great noise as the car door was being crunched. Jean never even left her word processor, and when I reported that it was going to cost $475 to fix it, she just smiled and said, "Oh, well. It could happen to anyone."

There has definitely been a change.

Carl Foster

INTRODUCTION

No one would be better at explaining how this book came into existence than the ones who, in January of 1985, gave me the assignment of writing a trilogy of truth books. These advanced spirits from the next plane of life, the Jesus Christ inspired Brotherhood of God, gave me the following message which I am using as the introduction to "Eternal Gold," the third book in *The Trilogy of Truth.*

"Teaming up with the writer was our first step in bringing these books to you, the reader. This entity, whom we know in this lifetime as Jean K. Foster, teamed up with us because she requested a teacher who would give her insight from this second plane of life. This entity knew that teachers often come to help individuals in the earth plane, to give them truth, to be the helpers they need to live their lives productively.

"The Brotherhood entered to speak to her through the process of writing, but she entered into communication with us very reluctantly at first. Teaming up was a matter of allaying her doubts which led her into debate with us."

Why the doubts, you may wonder. In the last chapter of this book, *The Opening of a Mind,* I explain how the communication began and why I hesitated in the beginning about accepting these advanced spirits into my life.

The Brotherhood continues. "When her doubts were laid to rest at long last, she began her work with us. Now this writer opens her mind to us fully, not holding back, not wanting her own thoughts to supersede those that make this book possible.

"The tender truth that this spirit entered into helped her to get her own life in order to allow her the peace of mind necessary to write. That was our first order of business—to counsel with her spirit self to help her work out problems. Then we helped her to enter into God-mind to receive the truth that pours out in torrents to become the books that we, the writer and this Brotherhood, write together.

"The Brotherhood of God was established by those advanced ones in the spirit realm who want to help those in earth life to become one with God. That is why we exist. The one you know as Jesus, who entered the scene over 2000 years ago, is our mentor, our inspirer. This writer teams up with us to aid in the work of helping those who call us.

"The theme of the book "Eternal Gold," is the teaming up with God-mind truth and putting it to work in the marketplace of life. The marketplace is that outer demonstration that you eternalize with the power of God, your Partner, to bring your truth into action. This action is the wellspring that brings you all that your heart yearns for.

"The book opens the reader to thoughts that will turn him or her to greater concepts of the God of the Universe—to tenderness, to prosperity, to wholeness, to energy that never runs out, to talent that develops to the utmost. Therefore, when you read this book, throw back the curtains that you pull across your embedded beliefs, and team up with this new enlightenment, this partnership with the open channel truth."

CHAPTER 1

TRUTH IN THE MARKETPLACE

The Spirit [handwritten] ~~Brotherhood~~ of God tells me over and over again, "Open your mind and open your heart that you will understand and make use of the truth that now comes to you." Now I say the same thing to you, the reader, who wants God truth to manifest as experiences and as material objects in your present lifetime. ~~Truly open your mind to the wisdom that the Brotherhood of God, through the God-mind connection, brings to you in this book.~~

"In this third book of *The Trilogy of Truth,* * we, the ~~Brotherhood~~ Spirit [handwritten] of God, bring you the third eminent truth that you need to understand and to use if you want the *eternal gold* that will enhance the teamwork between you and the powerful God of the Universe. Enter, then, to receive this truth, to bring it into your open mind where you will team up with all it means.

"*~~Truth, properly understood, must team up with earth substance.~~* This law, or principle, works within each person, not because the person has high or lofty ideals, but because the law is the law! ~~To be certain the truth that God-mind brings will not wither in the recesses of your mind, you must bring it~~

---

*Jean K. Foster, *Trilogy of Truth:* "The God-Mind Connection," 1987; "The Truth that Goes Unclaimed," 1987; "Eternal Gold," 1988; Kansas City, Uni-Sun.

forth as substance that is seen, heard, touched and otherwise understood by those in the earth plane."

The Brotherhood of God is a group of advanced spirits from the next plane of life who help me to make a connection from my mind to the mind of God. This God-mind connection is not just for me, however. It is for you, the reader. The good news about communication with the Brotherhood and with the Source of All Truth, the God of the Universe, is that everyone may have the joy and the benefits of it.

"God truth," the Brotherhood continues, "is the *eternal gold* that you can spend in your lifetime on earth. And furthermore, the gold, or God truth, may be spent on earth things without fear of it running out. You can count on *eternal gold* as that which will bring your best dreams into manifestation and bless others too.

"There are many who are amazed that their God truth is expressed in the earth plane. They accept wonderful things in their lives as mere accidents, not the results of what they hold in their minds as truth.

"There is more than one kind of truth, of course. There is earth-mind truth which is the collection of facts that are true, untrue, and even half true. This truth works to keep your mind centered in the earth itself as if it held the answer to whatever IS.

"The other truth is God truth, that which you can spend freely in the earth plane. 'Why, the greatest thing happened,' one may say to a friend. 'I had been thinking how wonderful it is that God is my perfect Source of good. I meditated upon this understanding. Then, without warning, great things came into my life. I got the job of my dreams, and I sold that property I had wanted to get rid of for years.' Unfortunately, this same person may look upon these events as a fluke, a sometime thing that probably won't be repeated.

"This chapter, 'Truth in the Marketplace,' has a message that you may find hard to truly accept. The message is—*the God truth you put within your being and become one with must manifest in the physical plane you live in.*

"Are you ready to put this truth to work? Will you put aside old beliefs in order to reap the benefits from the *eternal gold* that God-mind brings to you? Gentle presences surround you to help you to accept what is said here. They hold your truth in

the powerful teamwork of God, the Brotherhood and you. *spirit*
When you feel ready for this adventure we call 'Eternal gold,'
read further. Until then, work with what we have presented
thus far.

"The reader is the reason why The Trilogy of Truth was written. We bring to you the good news that Jesus and other great
entities have brought to earth—that God IS real, that God IS
what the great mystics have said. And we bring you the assurance that the God-mind connection is for each of you."

This first chapter continues with two parables to help us to
understand the message of "Eternal Gold."

"Here is a parable that might help you to understand the
way God truth is expressed in the marketplace of life," began
the Brotherhood. "There was a great truth that all the people
of a village accepted. This truth was that people could go to
the River of Life and get anything they wanted.

"One day, however, there came a person who questioned this
truth. 'Why do you think the river has the power to give you
anything? It looks like other rivers. Why do you call this particular river the River of Life?'

" 'Why, I got a gift there only last week,' said one. 'I wanted
gold to take to market to buy more good things for my little
home. When I went to the river, I asked for the gift, and when
I knelt down beside it, I could see the gold I wanted. I scooped
up what I needed, and I went my way.'

"The questioner thought a moment, and then he responded.
'The river bed undoubtedly has much gold. You need not have
asked for it. Anyone could go and take what he wants.'

"People looked at one another. They need not ask? They need
not wait beside the river to receive what they wanted?

" 'Take what you want,' the questioner told them. 'The truth
that you accepted for so long is not real.'

"The people ran to the river and began to work hard with
their hands to find the gold. Some found gold; others did not.
The gold began to peter out, and finally there was no more.
The river bed was scraped and penetrated, but all that appeared was mud. People went sadly back to their village because there was no more hope within them. The river was,
they decided, like other rivers.

"What is to be learned here? This story tells you that when
the truth of God is firmly fixed within you, nothing can stop it

from bringing forth into the material world whatever it is you want. But when you doubt this truth, stand it on its head and shake it for meaning, you turn great potential into an occasional wonderment that may or may not appear in the earth plane.

"Here is another parable that will bring clarity to the message. There was a man in the earth plane who arose early one morning. He stood at the door of his house and looked about his property. Entering into meditation, he spoke with the One he named the 'old One of heaven.'

"The old One teamed up with the man as soon as the thought went out that the man wanted to communicate. Then, without blinking an eye, the man in the doorway presented his problem for the day. 'My problem, old One, is that I cannot take the truth You teach as real. The truth sounds great, but when I work on my farm, I cannot see any relationship between that which You teach me and the world as I see it.'

"The old One approached the doorway. 'Turn to Me, friend. Turn to my Whole Being, not just part of it. Years ago I told you that the open truth of your being comes to you to be expressed in your life. Why is that hard?'

" 'That truth seemed great, old One, but I cannot put it to use in my life. Remember the truth You gave me about letting my spirit soar above the problems of life? Well, how can such truth help me to solve my farm problems?'

" 'That one is simple, friend of the land. To soar, you only have to ride in thought to the spirit that governs your land. Then, when you contact that spirit, you will learn how to put your crops into the ground, when to put them there, and you will learn how to care for them. Have you soared above the problems to meet the spirit of the land?'

"Shaking his head, the man pursed his lips. 'There is a spirit of the land? But why didn't you tell me this? You said to soar, and I tried, but I could not fly.'

"The old One stepped forward even closer to the man. 'Listen,' he said. 'I AM the gift and the giver, the part and the whole, the eternal truth and the personal truth. Why do you limit what I can do?'

"The man's eyes widened. 'Would you—could You—help me to hear the spirit of the land? Could You help me to soar above all my problems to the place where there are answers?'

"Tenderly the old One reached out His hand to the hand of the man. 'There is an answer, man of the land, that you have not found on your own. In My Being there is an answer for every question. Why wonder about the way truth opens itself to you? Why worry over what you think I may have meant here or there? Why turn and twist on the head of a pin?

"The old One continued. 'The answer to your questions, whatever they are, lies within My wisdom, My total understanding which I tenderly share with you. Therefore, enter your questions about the land, your questions about your life experiences, your questions about how you and I can be total teammates in your endeavors.'

"The man stood amazed. 'Why did I not understand earlier? Why did I think You spoke only once to people everywhere? Why did I think Your words were meant to be only for those with great spirituality? Why, I am just a man among men, a farmer who wants to team up with good ideas. Why would I merit Your attention?'

"The old One crouched in the grass beside the doorstep and looked up at the man. 'Trust Me. I AM what I AM.'

"The two of them—the man in the doorway and the old One who now crouched on the grass—teamed up in that next moment. The man crouched beside the old One, and together they spoke of the man's concerns. Together they stood. Together they walked down the path to work in the fields, to enter into great exchanges of their beings. The man, open and receptive, was full of questions. The old One, whose listening ear turned to hear everything that was said, placed His hand on the farmer's shoulder now and then as if to reassure him. Together they walked. Together they talked. Together they worked and entered into decisions.

"We hope you understand this story that shows man and God in open communication. Why worry over the meaning of scripture that came so long ago when you can ask questions now and receive answers from the One Who IS?

"To learn more about *eternal gold*, you need only talk with the Source of such gold, the God of the Universe. To gain this communication, you must team up with those who will help you to build the open channel into God-mind, that wonderful center of truth.

"Give the Brotherhood your open mind and your open heart

that you will not deny yourself the opportunity to put the God-mind truth into your own spirit self. Team up with us now by asking for or assenting to our help. Then enter into the pure and wonderful truth that God-mind pours out for you.

"Team up with the Brotherhood to receive the *eternal gold* of which we speak. Give your God self the thought that it is possible to have this gold, and it is possible to spend it in the marketplace of life. Make this thought one with your being by emptying earth-mind truth that injects thoughts of turmoil and doubt. Instead of earth-mind truth, use the Pure Truth that God-mind gives you—that *eternal gold* is the entire truth of prosperity.

"Now you are ready to enter your *eternal gold* into the marketplace. The truth that enters your being through the open channel provided by the Brotherhood will give you only the Pure Truth for your spirit, no one else's. It comes from God-mind to your mind, and it is that which you want to store within you so you can then express it in this lifetime experience. Remember, the truth that you expect to demonstrate in making your dreams come true is what we call *eternal gold*.

"Into this transaction comes the truth that we bring through this writer. We help her to make this connection and to bring her own mind into alignment with the Divine Mind of God. We will also help you, the reader, to enter into this connection. Yes, we will aid you who ask for help to make the God-mind connection yourselves so you can receive your own individual and perfect truth that God has just for your own soul.

"Therefore, the truth that you bring into your mind/soul and make your own is the *eternal gold* you are to use to produce the outer material in the earth plane. Yes, your truth goes into the earth plane as surely as the tender God of the Universe teams up with your being.

"No one who reads these words teams up with earth truth, surely! But if you still cling to those remnants of earth-mind truth that produce doubts within your thinking, now is the time to ferret them out into the open where you can see them for what they are. Earth truth is not only better left alone, it is dangerous to those who want to put the better truth—God truth—into their world.

"God-mind elevates your vibrations so that you may take the Pure Truth that enters your being and produce good from it.

But earth-mind reduces your vibrations into those that hold you fast to the earth itself. Therefore, no matter what great inspiration you may derive from God-mind truth, if you persist in the earth-mind truth, too, you will never demonstrate very much that is wonderful beyond compare. Low vibrations only take you to the edge of greatness, but then you are left to wither on the vine."

"You speak of vibrations," I interrupted. "Could you clarify what you mean?"

"Those of you who have raised your spirit to the God-mind connection have brought your vibrations into a high level," came the response. "The high level vibrations will connect into other high level vibrations, such as that which God IS. Yes, God enters into high vibrations, and therefore, when we put our beings into high vibration, we can better team up with all that is God.

"Now you understand that to put your truth, your Pure God Truth and the eternal truth, into the marketplace of life, you must become a person who devotes time to the project. 'Is it worth the time?' you may wonder. 'Is it necessary for me to produce truth since I have pretty much what I want in life?'

"We want to make a statement concerning this subject. That which God-mind brings to your mind is the only valuable asset that you truly possess! Those things you buy with the coin of the realm have no eternal value. They enter into corruption, do they not? They break, tarnish, fade from worth; isn't that right? Then why would you hold such things as more important than the truth that God brings you which can endlessly produce whatever it is you want?

"Now you must surely understand. Now you must want to bring your Pure Truth into manifestation in the earth plane. To have the Source is to have what mankind would risk all to have. But you, dear reader, must only give your time and your thought to the venture of using your truth to project whatever is needed or wanted into the earth plane.

"This book will open the doors of your mind to reveal all those recesses where you have stored earth truth. Never mind that you will stand revealed in this way. Team up to bring all into the open light of God. Then you will be able to fill your mind with the thought, the truth, the means by which you will live and work with God truth entirely."

I asked if the chapter was now complete. "There is one more point we wish to cover," the messenger from the Brotherhood answered. "The gentle truth that is here to become precious earth substance is ready to work in your life." Therefore, do not heed any distractions. Give the exactness of what we say to your being who is now ready to act upon its orders. The law says truth must express, and the being that you are will now allow the truth to obey this law.

"But if you, even now, turn to earth-mind truth for one more review, you will thwart the goal. Earth-mind, remember, lowers the vibrations, and there you will be with your wonderful truth out of synchronization with that which is God. Then the law is neutralized. Therefore, no one who wants to demonstrate, having put his hand to the plow, looks back."

Startled, I recalled Jesus' words in Luke 9:62. "No one who puts his hand to the plow and looks back is fit for the kingdom of God."

A commentary came very quickly. "The kingdom of God he mentioned is that state of being in which people proclaim their oneship with the God of the Universe. Those he thought were ready to go forth brought objections which were the old earth-mind truth. Jesus told them to let go, team up with the One Who could make their truth become whatever was needed and desired.

"Jesus knew, as you must know, that there is only one Source, one Teammate, one Tender Being who alone makes your truth team up with earth substance to meet your needs, whatever they are. Teaming up with God was then, and is now, the way to bring total optimum energy into the earth to become that which gives sustenance, which gives plenty and which presents you with the answers to your heart's desire.

"The tenderness with which we regard our offer to help you make your demonstration goes to you, the reader. The optimism which we team up within your beings must now produce great communication. The thrust of your generous truth will team up with the earth substance to become the answers that your questions seek.

"The truth is ready; you are ready; the God of the Universe is ready. The time is here to unite truth with earth substance. *Eternal gold* is now ready to be spent by you who are the generous extensions of God's own spirit."

CHAPTER 2

HOW TO MAKE TRUTH ETERNAL

I walk in the early morning. My two dogs, a golden retriever and a mixed terrier, frolic alongside, eager beyond canine expression to get to our destination—an open field with a stand of trees beyond. Once in the field, the dogs run free. I watch these four-legged friends with pleasure as I tramp along behind them.

My breath becomes deeper and deeper, my busy thoughts drop away, and finally I am centered in a grand physical exertion. We follow our well-worn path to the far end of the stand of trees where a broken-down fence outlines a lovely meadow. The retriever sails effortlessly through an opening and races out to investigate every scent. The terrier hops through the same space but turns in a different direction. For fifteen minutes or so I stand listening to an inquiring owl, the noisy clatter of bluejays, the clear tones of a cardinal, and many more bird songs I cannot identify.

I turn within to receive truth through the open channel the Brotherhood of God helps me to build. Words of wisdom pour through my mind from God-mind, words that help me in the living of my life, words that give me perfect and absolute truth for my own spirit growth. I am caught up in the experience. Though there is no need to walk to that particular place to receive God-mind truth, the walk itself helps me to quiet my mind so I can receive what the Source of Wisdom has to give me.

This chapter explains how we can work with the Brother- *spirit-* hood of God to get God-mind truth and then permanently in- stall it within our spirit selves. Once this eternalizing is done, we will use our truth in the marketplace of life as our *eternal gold."* *Spirit*

The Brotherhood continues. "We bring you the tender truth that comes through God-mind. ~~By 'tender' truth we mean it is not the 'old' truth, not the truth that people tell to one another of the accepted way.~~ Team up with us, those who enter earth plane whenever you call and who team up with you at your request. We who are the Brotherhood of God are eternal mes- sengers, advanced spirits, entering helpers who come when- ever you invite our presence.

"This teamwork we enter into brings you the open channel through which the God of the Universe gives you what is truly yours. This is what we do here in this next plane of life, team up with you who want Pure Truth that God-mind affords.

"~~By choosing the truth you want to direct your goals, your ambition, your whole lifetime experience, you are ready to lay your lifetime bet, so to speak.~~ This bet is laid out along with others that are put into the pot. Your bet either wins or loses depending on how well you read your hand.

"~~The one who wants to win depends on inner understanding and knowledge, so this person calls on the God-mind connec- tion.~~ But others, less wise, depend on the truth of the earth, the truth that mankind calls 'tried and true.' The bets win or lose depending on their innate value, right? Which do you think will win, the truth that God-mind presents or the truth that earth-mind gives? There is no contest!

"~~In order to lay a bet that will win against all odds, use the Pure Truth that God-mind has. Bet your entire purse or bank- roll on the truth from God-mind, for there is no way you can lose.~~

"Now work with the fervor of one who knows his bet will win, for in this way, you will cement the truth into your being. The Pure Truth is that which you put into your being and then work to eternalize, or make permanent. Once you have eternalized truth by the positive force of your acceptance, it will act within your being. The eternal truth will be spent as *eternal gold* to attain a lifetime experience beyond all your earthmind hopes and dreams.

"Our best projection for you is that there is a way to make God-mind truth permanent, indestructible, imperishable. Teaming up with this truth will lead your body into wholeness and perfection. Also, you will have generous thoughts of prosperity, and our teamwork will create your truth into the outer domain, your lifetime experience.

"Give your mind now to the work of accomplishing this. The way to become permanently imbued with this truth of God-mind is to wrest the old truth from your being. Hold the new thoughts in mind. Hold them there with the determination of one who has bet his entire stake on the game. Never take your mind from them. Put these thoughts uppermost in your mind because they must take hold and become permanently installed there.

"Put these thoughts within your spirit self. Lead them to your Pure Mind that connects to God-mind. Care for them with love, with gratitude, with the persistent thought of eternalizing them within you."

I asked how we know when the truth has eternalized so that we can quit the intense preoccupation with truth thoughts?

"Giving the thoughts to the spirit self eternalizes them within the time it takes to put all this down on paper. That is the greatness of God within the Universe that empowers you to do this wondrous thing—to put the new God-mind truth into your being. Teaming up with this truth and making it eternal is the process, and if you know the process, then doing it is simple. That is why we outline it here."

I asked what will happen if we don't enact the process described.

"If you miss the opportunity to eternalize the God-mind truth, the truth enters you to be a great inspiration which will fade in time. The eternalizing is what is important if you are to enact the pure truth from God-mind. The thought process is one thing. The eternalizing is something else. You, the reader, team up with a multitude of thoughts that enter you daily. But you do not eternalize them all. You put many of them on 'hold.'

You may want to reexamine the thought, the truth that seemed important at first. Perhaps it fades away with time. Then, the truth you once had within you is not there, but you can be sure that something else will take its place. The mind will always be full of thoughts, thoughts made permanent by the same process we describe.

"Perhaps you did not realize the control your spirit self has over this process. The way to belong to God-mind truth is to determine that this process will take place. Use your power of thought—the most important and powerful process in the universe. But use it rightly. Use it to get yourself into the flow of the energy of the God of the Universe."

I asked for an orderly review of the steps by which we get truth from God-mind and make it permanently ours.

"First, team up with the God of the Universe by going to the Brotherhood to make the God-mind connection. This connection will then send the thoughts that will allow you to place your bet on the table of life.

"Second, when the thoughts are in place, and you know they hold the winning potential, you must not take your mind to other places, other sources, or you diminish the hand you hold. Your mind, with God's connection, must stay fixed upon the new thoughts which will rout the old and take them to the empty places of the universe to dissipate harmlessly.

"Third, as the new thoughts take hold, you will team up completely with God-mind thought. Your life will take on new energy, new purpose. Now you understand that the best has happened, and you eternalize these thoughts. But when this happens, you empty out the old forever. The hand is still on the table, and your bet enters a new phase.

"Fourth, the person who bets the hand throws out the bet to the One who holds the pot, the One who will give out the winnings, the One who wants personal responsibility to be yours. Now this One says to you, 'Think what you want most in this world. Think it clearly.' The good truth enters to help you. The one who bets, you, considers the goal, the object, the purpose or whatever. The One holding the stakes, the One Who knows all there is to know, tells you to make a choice: either stay in the game or fold.

"The fifth and final step is either to stay in the game or to fold. It sounds simple, does it not? But the process is not sim-

- 12 -

ple unless you again rely on God-mind truth wholeheartedly to lead you past the point of indecision. When the test is over, when you elect to stay in the game, thoughts of Pure Truth eternalize forever more, and you go on to enact your heart's desire which your spirit entered life to accomplish."

The five-part process did not seem like a quick procedure to me. Yet, the Brotherhood said it can be done as quickly as it takes to read it.

"Those who team up with us will enter into the process easily because we will lead them to open their minds to it. The rest may need to approach the process again and again before they can accept it and enter into the procedure.

"Teaming up to eternalize your truth holds you to the mark until the process is complete. But remember, this process is *not* the penalty, it is the *opportunity.* This fact must be understood right here at the outset. The opportunity is here for you to make use of. But the God of the Universe does not penalize. He does not make you lose your bet. The God of the Universe *is* the Opportunity, the Great Power, the Great Thought. But He does not decide your purpose. Only you do this. Only you take or not take the truth that is pure and absolute for your soul."

I asked for an example of someone in the earth life who worked with making truth permanent within his spirit entity.

"There was a man who grabbed the truth when it first came to him, but he was so excited about it that he told everyone. Then others got excited too. 'Heaven was certainly smiling upon him,' they thought. Then they wrote and talked and in other ways made this truth wonderful to those who had never heard it. But they did not eternalize the truth within them, within their very inner selves, the indestructible part of themselves.

"They used their brains, they said. They used their own good sense, they told others. They took the wonderful individual truth that came to *one person* and multiplied it over and over to be the truth for all. Yet even the first person to receive it did not make it permanent within him because he didn't understand that he had an inner self, that there is only one reality, one permanent being, the wonderful spark of God Himself, his own spirit.

"Therefore, he thought in 'body terms.' He thought with his brain, he told others, and people worshiped their brains. 'I think with my own mind,' he said, not realizing that mind and brain are two separate things. The mind is of the spirit and the brain is of the body, you see. Therefore, this person and the others he affected entered into a kind of belief group that took truth from the one person, the guru, the one who supposedly had the key to heaven. But this person had no key save that which we all have.

"He teamed up with this first bit of truth, but he did not eternalize it within himself. Therefore, he clung to the old beliefs, and eventually the conflict between the old and the new destroyed his new-found excitement about truth. This often happens. People get insight, the touch of truth, then they do not make it permanent within themselves and eventually lose it. Others, seeing these lives, think that truth is not particularly advantageous. They see what they see, but they do not see rightly."

Many today warn of cults, systems of worship that inculcate an extravagant attachment to a person or a principle. I asked if what they said about following the truth of a guru is a reference to these cults.

"Cults are not new. They have been present in the civilization of the earth plane for centuries. They team up with whatever the entity who leads wants to present as truth. They enter the scene today as the usual thing, but they only present eternalizations that one person has. That is their weakness. Why rely on one leader, one truth presented by one person or one church? The point we make is to open your mind to Pure Truth that God-mind presents, not to truth presented by *any* one person.

"The matter of entering into someone else's truth is not the best for you, no matter where you get it. The cult is one thing that you mention, but there are other ways people buy into truth of those who go before them. Why do this? Why turn to others? Get the truth from God, the only Source in the Universe to present you with what you need and want for your own soul. Team up with this wonderful God whom we present here as the All in All, the Wonderful One, the Perfection, the Most Eternal Being, the Power and the Tenderness combined. What more could one want than this alignment? No cult, no church, no Bible, no truth that comes to you through others is as worthwhile as that you enter into when you team up with the God-mind connection."

Returning to the allegory about the bet, I asked if those who win the bet are to live out their truth in prosperity, health, achievement, joy and love.

"This question shows you understand the whole thing we say here. This is the way, yes! The bet is just a way to illustrate the message we bring, a way to show people how God-mind truth enters into them, how it becomes powerful, stable, permanent. Then they will not worry that 'God has left them,' or that 'God no longer wants good in their lives,' or that 'temptations may cause the whole God-thing to disappear.'

"That final step of eternalizing the truth within them is the key that unlocks the mystery of the ages, the key to working well with the Pure Truth of God. No one need fall by the wayside. Preachers will have to get a new subject with which to harangue people—something other than temptation and evil. For with the eternalizing of God truth within us, we will be invulnerable."

I asked if this was the method Jesus used to resist temptation so successfully?

"Teaming up with the Brotherhood, Jesus kept on the track he intended to follow when he took up residence within the baby form. Jesus turned to us to learn, and then he applied the truth of his own being to his own soul. Yes, he used this process to make the truth eternal within him. Therefore, he became a great person on earth. Jesus enacted his inner self in physical form so that people could see him, understand his words, become eager to enter into the same eternalizing that he did.

"Get yourself into this mode, this way of becoming one with God truth, and there will be no way to lose your bet. Team up with us now, with the Brotherhood who await only your thought of wanting our help. We come, we enter, we become the teammate who will help you to connect with God-mind truth.

"Teaming up with us brings your truth through God-mind. Then it is up to you to make this truth permanent within your being. This will be the way to place your bet. Giving yourself over to this process will put you into the flow of the Greatness of the Universe, the Almighty, the Tremendous, the whole Thought-Principle teaming up with your own inner self. Then the bet is secure, teamed up with the only One who can make the entire pot or stake become yours.

CHAPTER 3

TEAMWORK—THE BASIC PROCESS

spirit

"Never wait until the *perfect time* to team up with the Brotherhood. Teaming up can take place even as we write this sentence. Therefore, decide now to receive the valuable teamwork that will boost your ability to call forth the eternalized truth into the marketplace."

spirit

This is the warning the Brotherhood has given me many times about how easy it is to procrastinate in the matter of spiritual growth. "People want to try out an idea, hold it in their minds, talk it over with others. Then they eternalize whatever other people have said about it, instead of trying the idea out for themselves." Therefore, this chapter begins on an urgent note to team up with the Brotherhood to get the God-mind connection.

"We talk to you now about teaming up because it is the only way to manifest the eternalized truth within you. Working with the Brotherhood will call forth this truth, and it will manifest into the physical nature that is your world. Therefore, we must take this matter up with you so you may demonstrate truth in the outer or physical world.

"There is no limitation. Getting the perfect demonstration is only a matter of understanding how to team up and how to use the right thoughts.

"Here is the way it works. First, get the God truth into your inner being. Second, eternalize this same truth. Finally, you must team up with us to get at the heart of the matter, the demonstration of the inner truth into the outer world.

"Now make teamwork the foremost thought in your mind. Teamwork is you working with this Brotherhood through God-mind. Therefore, turn to us to make the connection. It is only a matter of thinking, 'I want to join with this Brotherhood to make the connection to God-mind.' In this plane thoughts are read with ease. In fact, this is how we communicate. So, when you know you have opened your mind to us, think of this Mind of God, this Mind that is the source of all Truth. Become one with the idea. Understand?

"Now put this idea, this thought, into the energy that surrounds you, the God energy that enters you when the God-mind connection is made. Then this energy pours forth to you. Many enter into a kind of ecstasy, and they simply empty out the energy rather than make use of it by entering it into their inner selves."

I asked what we are to do if we don't feel this energy pouring into us.

"When this energy comes forth, whether you 'feel' it or not, put your belief into it. Then enlarge the energy by putting the thought into your inner being that there is this endless supply available for you. Got that?

"This way you move step by step toward demonstration. Team up with these thoughts we have presented. Then you enter them with authority into your body self, your physical brain that awaits its orders. 'The body,' you say to it, 'is now energized with the energy which God puts here. This energy teams up with me entirely.' Then wait a while, and give your appreciation, your love toward this energy, this entire idea.

"Now for the final step: Form a picture in your mind of what you want. Never create a vague picture. Think in detail. Think in the eternal way with energetic thoughts that know they will be joined with the physical world. Never allow the doubts of earth-mind to creep in and be entertained within you. Those earth-mind thoughts only turn your best energy into that which enters into the universe for others to use. Therefore, put those thoughts out the window of your inner self, out in the vastness of the universe where God may purify them. Give them your full power to throw them out.

"Give yourself the test to see if you have done the things you must do to bring about the demonstration. One, have you entered the truth that comes to you from God-mind? If you are in doubt, review the first chapter, 'Truth in the Marketplace.' Two, eternalize the truth. Have you done this perfectly as outlined in Chapter 2, 'How to Make Truth Eternal?' If you are unsure, review the chapter. Three, eternalizing the truth makes it firm within you, and now it is time to put this truth to work in the earth plane. If you again feel unsure, review *this* chapter. Following a procedure is the only way to get yourself into the perfect alignment with God-mind to put the truth where it will demonstrate in the outer. The entire picture we present here is done step by step, but if you try to skip one step thinking you already understand it, then you may not make an easy demonstration.

"Never think that you enter into this process alone. We, the Brotherhood, go with you all the way. Therefore, know us, be our friend, team up with us to have our counsel and our advice. This may be done mind to mind, by entering into meditation with us. But first you must know we come to help you, never to lead you astray. Enter into our communication to straighten out any misconceptions, to get advice on your life, to reach the truth from God-mind. We stand here at the ready to help in all ways. We are that Brotherhood of Christ, that body of advanced spirits who works with Jesus to be the Counselor, the Comforter and the Holy Ghost, or Spirit that works through God to bring you eternal truths.

"Hold as important this entire business of making truth perform in the marketplace. There is no way to be one with God unless you work with Him, that God of the Universe, that Perfection, that Wonderful Truth, that Eternal Energy which God IS. Teaming up with us is your way to be at peace with the matter of God at work in your life.

"Many wonder how God actually works in their lives. Many think surely He is a person who has the eternal truth but who will not share it with them. Teaming up with a wonderful unlimited and non-judging God has not occurred to them. But there is eternal truth that goes forth to you whether you become aware of it or not. For example, the thought that persists within you to be or to do the wonderful, meaningful things is God talking to your spirit self.

"But most of the time the earth-mind truth wets down this wonderful truth by reminding the person that he is really an eternal idiot, or an eternal hopeless sinner, or the person without talent and so forth. That way the earth-mind truth keeps you from teaming up with God-mind truth. So, we always say over and over again, come with an open mind, an open heart and open your eyes to what is true in this universe. Push out the inadequate truth you have clung to from habit. Team up with the incredible, wonderful and perfect God-mind truth that helps you become the wonderful person you want to be.

"Getting into the flow of energy will help you to become more perfect, more tender, more energetic and whole. This energy is to be used, not put on the shelf to be admired like artifacts from the past. This truth comes to be used in the here and now. That is why we bring this message, to urge you to put this truth to work in your life. Team up!

"Now put the entire business of truth getting into the forefront of your being. What is more important, after all, than getting your life into energized perfection? This is the business at hand. This is the true eternal program that you came to earth life to align yourself with.

"Now turn your being toward the eternalization process once again. The truth that we give you in this chapter must be entered to work with your personal truth. There is the eternal universal truth, and there is the pure and absolute truth that comes to you through God-mind. These two truths, of course, enter from the same source, but the eternal universal truth applies to everyone while the pure absolute truth applies only to you.

"Team the truth we give you in this chapter with your inner being, the part of you that is incorruptible, the part of you that teams up with God-mind. When you have done this, *manifestation must take place.* This is, after all, the principle by which universal truth operates. The truth that you hold permanently within you must manifest in the earth plane.

"Never combine with truth that is inferior. The inferior truth will lead you on to many goals, but it will eventually leave you in the pits of despair. Teaming up with inferior truth will not take you far enough toward your permanent goals."

I asked for examples of permanent goals.

"Tender thoughts that arise within you to team up with your being are permanent goals. These will try to lead you to do great things with your life, they will often lead you to take big chances emotionally, and they will team you up with high ideals that you wish to manifest. Thoughts of greatness—these are the permanent goals that your inner being, your very soul will want to make manifest.

"Inferior truth will lead you to inferior goals. Owning your own house, for example, is not a bad goal, but it is inferior as the overall goal for your life. The goal of inferior truth is usually only a physical goal such as attaining property, developing power by earthly standards or money that will buy nothing of permanent value. Inferior goals perish and rot away.

"The goals of lasting value are those things that do not rust or corrupt. Therefore, these goals may be the founding of helpful institutions, the eternalizing of values in various ways. These values may be demonstrated in alignment with those things that will help people establish personal values such as goodness, purity of soul or purity of body. These may be teamed up with the physical values too, of course.

"The permanent goals of your soul rise above the mundane thoughts of the good life, above the thoughts that people often entertain to give themselves pleasure. These permanent goals present challenges to those who accept them, but they also present the greatest opportunities to be the enactment of truth in this lifetime. These goals enter you to be challenges, not passing thoughts.

"Those who enter these thoughts within themselves rise above the inferior truth of personal material goals and reach great heights. Now open your eyes. Now open your mind. The truth of the ages, the truth that enters you through God-mind, is that truth which brings you into oneness with the God of the Universe. Then you will have that lifetime experience that will take you to great heights both in the earth life and in the next plane.

"No one will be disappointed who takes on these great creative thoughts. No one will have regrets. The great truths persist anyway, and see how much better it is to team up with God-mind to bring them into manifestation rather than let them go by while you pursue inferior truth!

"Never throw away your truth to those who do not understand it. Team up with God-mind in secret. Team up with what is most powerful, most wonderful, most energetic, but tell no one of this inner work. Team up but remain silent about the process when you talk to others. This way you work only with God Who will never let you down. This way you have the help of the Brotherhood whom you will lean on and trust.

"When you talk about the greatness of the God-mind truth within you, others will question, wonder, throw cold water on you. Never share what is your perfect understanding, because your perfect understanding is the teamwork that you have with us and God-mind. Throwing it to others will only weaken your own resolve and leave you open to their thoughts and expressions. That is why the perfection that each seeks must be done personally.

"Needs that you have, needs in your life such as perfection of body or mind, needs on the subject of prosperity, needs about your life and your relationships, these will be resolved by working with us. But *never* tell others about these resolutions or explain how they came about. This way you remain strong. This way God-mind will enter your own mind to team up with you. The teamwork must be done in secret and kept in secret. This inviolate rule will prosper the working out of your tender thoughts, but the sharing of this truth will only weaken it.

"Now work out your inner truth. Team up with us to receive help as you need it. We will always be there to help, be there to advise, be there to comfort."

CHAPTER 4

HOW THE DEMONSTRATION PROCESS WORKS

spirit

The ~~Brother~~hood of God makes a statement about demonstration that may boggle your mind. Or, if accepted fully, it will open the door to the achievement of all your good desires and goals. "When you do what you want, get the truth from God-mind and become one with it, you will demonstrate whether you realize what is happening or not. *spirit*

"The process will work because it must," the Brotherhood says. There are no qualifications to this accomplishment, you will notice. God is not judging our characters or deciding who is deserving of this demonstration. Some may be put off by this lack of judgment, believing that only deserving people should demonstrate truth. "This is erroneous," says the Brotherhood. "The truth enters people to make them partners with God— one with true Perfection, true Eternal Good. There is no judgment needed when people team up with the truth from God-mind."

"In this plane where the spirit enters after earth life, we communicate by thought, you know. Though the thought process is not hard to understand, it is hard to get used to when you have been in a body on earth. The body eternalizes the thoughts that go forth, and then the spoken word appears.

This method of communication gets to the point very slowly. But the communication process which we use here goes as fast as the thought itself.

"Communication is not the only difference between the two planes. The body enters into union with those faculties that you call sound and sight. There are, of course, various levels of sound, pitch and tone, but none of these body faculties can compare to the thought process that gives you these things plus much more variety. The body is limited, you see. Every composer knows this when he writes music. Every painter knows this when he attempts to paint what he sees not only with his outer eyes but with his inner eyes. No paint brush, no colors can really express what this painter has in mind.

"Thought, the misunderstood process. Yes, thought is not given its share of credit. The thought we speak of enters our minds in a flash, even faster than the computer works when you press the 'Enter' key. The thought goes to you and from you with the speed of the universal tension, and no person can calculate that speed. Never think that your thoughts are inferior to the spoken word. Not so! First, there is the thought. Second, there is the expression in the physical. This way the inner person is the controlling force, not the body self.

"Teaming up with us, as we have indicated, is the process of thought, only thought. There is no bodily alliance here at all, no entering into some peculiar kind of oneness with us. The Brotherhood is composed of those who have advanced both on earth and in the further planes of life. We work together, and we work separately to reach all of you who want our help to connect to God-mind. Team up with us now to realize the wonderful potential of our working together. Then we will demonstrate the truth with you in an experiment. This experiment will take you into the use of your mind, your thought process. Team up to make this happen, to make this demonstration unify with the thought you hold in mind.

"New thoughts come fast into your mind now. They touch upon the endless possibilities here. Good! And there may be some of you—there usually are some—who touch upon their fears here. They turn away because they think, 'This is witchcraft!' or 'What if this is of the evil spirit?' But there is no spirit save that of the powerful, wonderful and great God of the Universe. Team up with this God, and your fears will dissipate because your innate being will present thoughts from God-mind that teach absolute truth.

"Never throw away an opportunity to demonstrate. Team up with this process in order to become entirely dependent on the Real Source, the Pure Substance which comes from the universe, from the God who gives it to you. Team up with this process that you may make more and more demonstrations to give your truth its proper place in your lifetime experience. Then your spirit will grow, will soar, will team up with all that God IS.

"Now let us get to the demonstration. Team up with us here. Team up with us who lead you to this pure and wonderful moment when you will demonstrate the truth within you. Get the entire focus of your being into this work. Now direct your thought to the following explanation.

"New thoughts now team up with your being. Never turn them away, no matter how far-fetched. Point the thoughts into your inner mind, the mind that can be their filter. They flow around you, opening new ways of life, new ways of directing your expressions. These thoughts swirl with vigor because they enter you on the whirlwind of God-mind, that energetic force that brings you every creative thought. Yes, send the thoughts to your inner mind which is connected to God with our help. Give us your energy, your pure trust. We, here in this Brotherhood, reach forth to you. You, there in your inner being, reach forth to us. We unite in spirit to bring these thoughts into each process known to you as demonstration.

"Now the thoughts will settle down within you that you may examine them. You are ready to demonstrate some of them, but others will not tempt you because you are not prepared for advanced work. Therefore, pick that thing, that thought that you are comfortable with. Hold it. We give it our approval, though our approval is not needed here. We do this simply to encourage you to guide this thought into demonstration. Give the thought that you want to demonstrate the push that it needs to enter into the pure energy of God. *Team up with this idea.*

"Push this idea into the universal substance, letting it team up with what God provides you. Get into the flow here. The teamwork is working right now. The thought is concrete, is it not? The thought has dimensions, does it not? The thought has the result in mind, does it not? Then you know it demonstrates. Getting this thought into energy is the business of God-mind. Your business is to push it out there and see the dimensions and the result that you expect. Think. Think of that dimension, that result you want, that pure intention that wants to make the best demonstration ever known.

"Now put the truth of this demonstration on the inner shelf of your mind. Put this beautiful, well-defined thought on this newly created shelf within you where the thought will manifest into a beautiful outer demonstration. Entering this well-defined thought into your inner temple is very important here. Put it there, pat it, appreciate it, know that it is a gift from the God of the Universe Who has many gifts to give. This God of the Universe never withholds these gifts because of judgment upon those who want the gift. He never declares that you are unworthy. God of the Universe is a Giver, not a Taker. He never touches lives in order to teach lessons that make the people unhappy. Therefore, team up with this wondrous concept of God while you appreciate the gift that is in the process of demonstration.

"Now—go about your life knowing that you have this pregnant thought that is entering into demonstration. The pregnancy—the beautiful thought which has dimension and has a result in your mind—teams up with the powerful forces which you acknowledge. The God of the Universe wants to bring you into the demonstration to free you from error thinking, to make you the wondrous creature on earth that you are intended to be.

"Team up with the Brotherhood to make this demonstration the sort that leaves no doubt in your mind that it comes as a result of the process we have described to you. Team up with us to put aside your own petty concerns. Those things that irritate, those thoughts that would invade to enter doubt, the teamwork of others who will not understand and who stay only to irritate and to confuse—give those things no resting place within you. Put them away.

"Remember, do not share your innermost demonstration with anyone. When you have made demonstrations over and over and you then know the confidence of the advanced soul, you can teach others what you have learned. The teaching is not easily done, and it only occurs if a student wants what is taught, asks for it, actively seeks it. Therefore, never be concerned if you cannot teach eternal truth to others. Why work at this? Those who want it will reach for it. That is sufficient.

"Your demonstration is under way. The teamwork of this Brotherhood works with your own inner being to enter this wonderful well-defined thought of yours into the earth plane. There! It emerges. We can see it entering into the physical now. Direct your thoughts toward this. Now send the thought to the Great Source of all power, the God of the Universe. How much greater can you think? We give you this concept of God to contemplate that you might stretch your mind, stretch your growth into the bigger teammate. We see your growth from here. We reach forth to touch your hand, to encourage you in this growth. Give us your partnership, your understanding, your confidence. We, you and we, will work together with the God of the Universe to demonstrate the great thoughts that enter your mind.

" 'Wonderful,' you say? Well, we want to assure you that there is so much more to this growth that you will be amazed, and you will be partners with the tremendous powerful energy that teams you up with all that is God. Would you want more than this? Never hesitate, never throw away this opportunity. Enter into our experiment with the fervor of one who just entered into a love affair. The blood runs strong, does it not? The thrill of joy courses through the system that is the body, does it not? Health appears greater than it has ever been, does it not? There is strength in your muscles that you have never fully realized, right? All things seem possible, right? The love you have for a person and the love that person has for you reaches through your entire being to raise you into the higher, most wonderful level of physical expression. That is demonstration!

"That is what you do here with our demonstration. You begin with the thought that enters you through God-mind to be something that is especially for you. Then the thought goes into the inner mind where you refine it, give it dimension, give it a concept of the pure result intended. Then you place it on the shelf of your mind, in that glowing, energetic substance which God provides you. There the idea begins to take shape. Your mind refines it even more if it is needed, and then, presto, just like the baby's head shoves through the birth canal, there is the thought made manifest.

"Be into the whole demonstration, not a part. Do not stop short of producing your thought in the physical world. Do not be satisfied with only a great thought. Team up now with one who wants you to make a demonstration. He is the Brother of Brothers, Jesus, who entered into life to be the complete demonstration, and who wants you to make this demonstration now.

"Send the pure thought that you have the teamwork that is needed to enter into demonstration relying on the encouragement that Jesus himself gives you. He is the one-with-God spirit which you, which all of us want to be. Your demonstration is part of being one with God, but it is not reserved for the few. This demonstration is meant for the many. Therefore, reach out with your mind and renew the thought that you want to demonstrate. Team it up with the largest concept of God that you can manage. Then give the thought dimension, give it its result. Then the person that you are will know the oneness with God that will enlarge your gentle spirit and enter the thought into demonstration.

"New thoughts will continue to come to you when you connect with God-mind. They are the creative flow of ideas that enter to be your very own, and they compose the pure truth that is designed for your own soul growth. Therefore, never think any idea that enters through God-mind is too farfetched or over zealous or too ambitious. Thoughts that enter to be yours are *yours* indeed, and they are meant to be acted upon.

"The greatness that some achieve comes about because they pay attention to these thoughts, put them in their minds to be worked upon by themselves and by God. Then comes the demonstration. The thoughts provide the inner direction, the inner teamwork that goes forth to make you the perfect person you are supposed to be in this lifetime.

"Perfect? You may question that word. But the Brotherhood *spirit* knows that you came to your earth life with a plan, a plan that would make your experience perfect beyond your wildest thought. Therefore, why not enact it? Why not become that perfection in action? That is what demonstration is, perfection in action!

"Needs that enter your life may be the result of wrong thinking, the kind of thinking that expects the body to weaken, for example. Error thinking leads many to expect and even to welcome suffering because they think suffering makes them more pure and more Christ-like. But these thoughts are only errors, not the positive God force which makes dreams and goals come true. Why would people believe that God sends suffering to make one a better soul? The truth is just the opposite. God sends wholeness. The person must reach out for it, however. Wholeness is what we want you to expect, what we want you to become one with. Reach into your inner self and put the wholeness concept there. Then stand up with the best of the body temples and express this wholeness!

"Turn your mind now to the God of the Universe, to the One Who is the Reality, the Perfection, the Greatness. Now, what is your thought about this God? Give us your own thought, not someone else's. Direct to us your best idea of what God is. Be honest, not devious, because we read your thoughts anyway. Give us your pure thought no matter what it is. Then we can help you to extend the concept. This part, this process, is intended to strengthen your own concept of God that your demonstration might come about sooner.

"The *concept* is the key to how fast or how slow you will manifest your thought. The thought of God must reach out beyond the farthest reaches of the universe and beyond. But few understand such a description. Few understand that God is not just the Man in the sky, the Someone who enters to provide food and shelter and the tenderness of forgiveness. Few believe God is more than this.

"God—the Wonderful Vastness of Complete Good. Who can enter such a concept in his or her mind? God is the principle of Eternal Good, Eternal Power, Eternal Energy. Team this up in your mind with the thought you have of God. When you do these things, you enhance the demonstration, you become the mover of your thought to the vast energy of the universe. The God of the Universe then does the other part of molding the thought into the outer physical expression. "Now we leave this tender thought of demonstration for you to work on while we go forward to explain and to fulfill our own purpose in this book."

CHAPTER 5

LEARNING ABOUT JESUS' TRUTH

If you hold the Bible as the final authority on the truth and wisdom of God, this chapter may prove difficult for you. However, if you believe in the continuing revelation of God to mankind, you will be open to what you read here. Furthermore, since the Brotherhood of God is inspired by Jesus, who else but the Brother of Brothers could properly enlighten us about what he meant to teach during his lifetime experience two thousand years ago?

"Teaming up with the truth of the ages is what we are doing here," the Brotherhood begins. "The truth that Jesus is quoted to have given to men and women is in the Bibles that people read. But the truth that Jesus actually brought to people is not entirely that which the Bible quotes as truth. This chapter, therefore, is to be the correction, the positive identification of what Jesus' truth is and what it is not. The various ideas that people have regarding Jesus' truth are part of earth-mind thought, and thus team up with error thinking. Because people believe this error thinking, they lack the needed understanding of what Jesus came to teach.

"Work through this chapter by entering into the eternalization of the God-mind truth that you already have within you. This eternalization is what your spirit self works with to rise beyond the mere earth-bound truth. It is this poor truth that teams up with what people think and believe about God, the earth, themselves, the entire universe. But this truth is so limited that people can only rise to the beginning of what life can truly be, and then they stop. Unless they advance beyond the earth-mind truth, they will team up with what is entirely too inadequate.

"Never will people rise above the earth-mind unless they can identify it. They will always wonder which truth they accept in their inner temples—the earth-mind truth or the God-mind truth. That is the dilemma most people find themselves in. Therefore, they want the authority that says to them, 'This is the whole and entire truth here. Pay attention to this and you need never wonder what is truth again.' But of course they do wonder because their souls cry out for the absolute truth, the truth that does indeed pass all other understanding, the truth that rises so far above that which they have embraced before that they know they must be on the right track.

"This chapter also will cover your various needs—the need to live an abundant life, the need to enter into an eternalization of the truth which is for you, no one else. Tune in with an open mind to this entire truth, tune in with the open teamwork that embraces the God of the Universe, the unlimited and unlimiting God. Get into the flow of our truth here and listen, think, read, tend to your own spirit/mind that will know truth from untruth. Get yourself into this entire truth revelation.

"Here is that Brother of Brothers, the one you call Jesus of Nazareth. He will now talk to you of his lifetime on earth, his lifetime where he lived and where he died, the lifetime where he preached, where he demonstrated the truth that came directly to him through God-mind. This Brother of Brothers, this one whom we in the Brotherhood revere and love, will now address you."

JESUS SPEAKS TO THE READER

"Give me your entity, that spirit self of you who enters into the learning process we teach in this book. The entity that you truly are, the one that eternalizes truth and demonstrates in the physical lifetime is the one I must talk with here.

"Needs that enter your life, whatever they are, will not go unnoticed by this Brotherhood. These needs belong to our province of concern. They will not be just your needs, but *our needs*. Teaming up with the Brotherhood gives you the assurance that you will not meet anything in your lifetime experience alone. That is my truth. That is what I demonstrated in my own last incarnation when people teamed up with me in the part of the world that now is Israel.

"Never think that I came to earth to be a great leader as some thought. The idea of earthly leadership was not true, and those who believed in it were disappointed in me. Therefore, they turned against me. Those who entered into spiritual teamwork with me realized that I was in touch with the God of the Universe, and they heeded my words about how they could do the same as I. But they were unprepared to make this alliance without my physical presence, and they began to have doubts about our equal partnership, our being one and the same before God.

" 'How can I ever rise in bodily form?' they asked. 'How could I forgive my enemies?' they wondered. People's thoughts centered on the idea that they and I were not in the same eternal plan, and they became concerned. Therefore, they opened their minds to new thoughts which would explain their concerns. They, the followers, began to team up with the idea that because I spoke of myself as the 'Son of God,' I must indeed *be* God. They believed then that I came down from heaven to give them the plan of salvation, the plan of the new network of the Godhead. They emptied my truth, and instead, they presented their own understanding.

" 'Why,' they said, 'this Jesus teams up with us because he is God Himself. Now we understand! We must worship this person, this Jesus who is the incarnation of God Himself.' The whole thing got very complicated, and churches were established to sort out the truth of the matter. They sorted through the manuscripts, they listened to the oral history, but they did not go to the Brotherhood, the counselor, to learn the truth first hand. They took the first manuscripts, they altered them, they tried to put into the new writings this idea of Jesus as the *only* Son, missing the mark entirely. But they went ahead with all this, and no matter who weighed the evidence, they teamed up with the wrong ideas.

"Never was there any intention on my part to put myself before people as the God of the Universe. I told them of the loving nature of God to improve their own God concept, but I did not make myself God. They entered this thought after I left the earth plane, and then they undid most of my work there. Yes, they hold me in great regard, they celebrate what they call my birthday, but they do these things in error. The greatness that they wonder at is God within the person, the God of the Universe demonstrating His wonderful qualities through the entity which I AM. That is the certainty of the matter. And they knew I said that what I did they, meaning any of you, can do also. That is what I meant then, and it is what I mean now.

"Be the one to hold these truths self-evident, that God is God; I AM that spirit entity who made the demonstration of pure truth in my lifetime experience to bring hope to people. That is the pure and great truth here. Team up with me, this entity who came to earth life as the Jesus you hear so much about. Those who enter into the Pure Truth of God—that truth that comes through God-mind just for you—will understand what I am saying. They will not resist my truth here.

"But those who depend upon the outer truth that descends from the hierarchy of the churches or the books will mistrust what they read. They 'know' in their hearts that the only truth comes from the Bible, or perhaps from the Church. But they will not reach their eternal plan in this lifetime by heeding the observations of others, including the Bible. Hold *only* the truth in your inner self, in your inner being who enters the body to live this lifetime. Hold onto the truth that comes through God-mind, and your life will become that which pleases you because the teamwork of the Brotherhood, the God of the Universe, and your being will give you all that is needed to live a wonderful lifetime.

"Give yourself now to God-mind truth. Hold the inner self up in the eternal truth by giving your witness to the teamwork that comes to you and through you from God-mind. Know this wonderful truth and live a lifetime of confident partnership with God.

"Be into the perfection that gives your spirit self its growth which makes you the wonderful person who wants to be the son of God. The 'son' is the same as being 'one with God.' That is what 'one' is—the eternalization of the truth that God enters the individual entity and makes that entity a perfect child in thought, in lifetime experience.

"How has the thought process worked with you? Teaming up with the Brotherhood must be a startling experience that makes you realize that the teamwork is true, honest, that which will indeed make changes in your life. But if your thought process has gone into a stalemate, then you now must be reading only intellectually, not with the entire person. Never think that you will move ahead in growth if you enter into a stalemate. The thought of the wonderful teamwork with the Brotherhood must open you to new experiences, new thoughts, new inner work. Then your lifetime will abound with good as surely as the sun appears to rise in the morning. Get into a confident partnership with me as I try to team up with your being. Reach out to me, hold out your tender thought to me, to this entity whom you have so long misunderstood.

"Never did my disciples know entirely what the experience meant, but they were close to the truth. They were trying, they were reaching out their thoughts to expand their understanding. They wanted to bring others into the understanding, too, and then problems began. People had various beliefs, and getting new truth was hard for them. Therefore, those who were close to me in person or even in thought, wanted so much to convince others that I was the one-with-God they waited for, that they made my purpose different.

"The emperor of the Roman empire gave his sanction to Christianity, finally. But he was the one who completely misunderstood Christian thought, both before he gave the sanction and afterwards. He read a lot, he listened a lot, people served him their ideas, and he had an influence, overall, upon Christianity himself. The legalization of this religion was the final step in putting my experience into the teamwork of earth-mind truth. This earth-mind truth wanted religion to bring peace, so I became the Prince of Peace. They wanted those who ruled to be divine also, so they used Christianity to give a blessing to kings. They wanted the ordinary person, as they thought of people and classified them, to receive the orders, do the work, die for country and be generally unthinking; therefore, they tendered the Christian truth as absolute, and others presented it to those who could not read.

"They could think, they could pray, they could belong to the Brotherhood, but when they did this, they were branded heretics and were killed. The truth that Christianity brought into the world has been shallow indeed. But those who now go forth with individual truth may enter the true pronouncements, the true meaning into it. But do not wait for this act. You enter into the Brotherhood even as I did on earth, learn from them how to connect with God-mind, and then you will be the great receiver, the one who tends his truth with ardor, with the concern that a mother has for her baby. Then your soul will flourish.

"The truth that eternalizes within you will bring you great thoughts that others will want to share. Needs will disappear into satisfactions and into fulfillments. This eternal truth enters each person to eternalize what is needed by that individual spirit self to grow into the person who will be one with God. Teaming up is what it is all about in this lifetime experience—teaming up with the Brotherhood and teaming up with God-mind.

"Never throw the truth you receive from God-mind to those who may ridicule it. Why throw what is perfect to those who will not understand? They will only team up with those who know not what truth is. They will throw the eternal partnership concept out the window. But they know not, so you must not hate them. They do what they enter to do—nothing. They must have lost sight of their plans, and they know not how to get a plan together. The plan is there with your spirit self, and only God-mind may help you with it. The truth that enters you through God-mind will never let you down."

I asked at this point if this was still Jesus talking.

"This is indeed he. Gentle thoughts enter to help you explain all this to the readers. The thoughts (my questions based on scripture) from you to me also enter. But there is no way I will take the entire scripture word by word to explain it! The overall meaning of my life is what is important, not all the scripture. But if you need more revelation about me, ask."

At his invitation, I plunged in by saying, "In Christianity most emphasis is on the Easter celebration—the resurrection of your body when your disciples and others realized that death is not the end it appears to be. Do you agree that the fact of your continued life is most important?" Reluctantly, I excused myself here to answer the telephone. When I hung up, the message continued.

"Team up with me to understand what I say. The truth that I gave you before you left this machine stated the truth that I believe to be the most important. That people may live their lives with the God of the Universe as their Guide, their Mentor, their every Help, is what my life was all about. Eternal teamwork, that is the thing. This Brotherhood enters to give help, comfort, to encourage and to link the entity with Godmind. Then the individual is entered into the flow of divine ideas that come because those thoughts belong to that person. This truth is not sent just to impress or just to give entities a partnership with teamwork. It comes to be that partner, that everlasting perfect open channel that each entity needs to live his lifetime with power and understanding."

Again I asked a question. "What do you have to say about this: To be a Christian, people must accept Jesus as their savior, believe that he is the son of God, and confess their sins that they may be forgiven."

"This is error thinking. This is not true. People who want to be Christian, whatever that means, team up with this eternalization of truth in order to have the firm truth, or what they consider truth. They do believe in it, and they insist that others believe it too. But I did not institute this thing. Never confuse being a Christian with getting the absolute truth from God-mind. There is no way to enter God-mind truth into yourself by affirming the Christian eternalization. That people will team up with this idea is not to my mental understanding. The way to become one with God is to adhere to your own truth, not to the truth of others. Did I enter into the truth of others? The truth of others was Judaism, but the law made that life hard to follow. Therefore, I brought new concepts."

"You sound like you do not care for designations such as Christian, Jewish, Moslem, Buddhist," I commented. "Is this true?"

"Teaming up with such designations, as you call them, will not make a lifetime experience more worthwhile. The thoughts that these various religions, these church divisions, all the interpretations of the Bible present, will not make a lifetime experience one whit better. Why? Because you find yourself applying the truth of others to your own life, and it will not exactly fit. The one who entered to be the prophet that they named Christianity after did not want the designation of Christianity. He wanted to teach certain concepts. He wanted to enlarge the concept of God, first. Then he wanted to show people how to open their minds to hear the new words of God. The way he taught all this was by example and by words. But the words were to be the general observations, not the specific ones for each soul. The person of Jesus which I was, entered life to be the one who could demonstrate truth in his life. I did this, but when it was accomplished, I made the final demonstration of rising from the dead to teach people that there is no death, no entity who does not awaken.

"Therefore, the reason I came and the reason I am remembered are two different things. The sweet baby Jesus is not my reason for coming. Entering through the channel of the woman's body is the normal entry, is it not? The virgin birth was inserted material. I entered no thought about virgin birth. There was love and concern for the mother figure. This person was and is dear to me. It is important to know that relationships eternalize both on earth and here. But there is no less concern for the one who entered to be my father. He, too, was my concern in the earth life. But the two of them have become the eternal pageant that is reenacted year after year. This may bring the helpless baby feeling and the need of parents to the fore, but it has nothing to do with the idea of why God enters into our lifetime experience. This baby grew to manhood and had parents who received truth through God-mind so that they held to their own truth and kept themselves and me safe from enemies. But the truth is that anyone may do the same thing.

"The angels who proclaimed my birth? Well, I know of no such angels. But if they did, they also proclaim the birth of all of you. This wonderful plan that we come into the world helpless is the method that entities use to learn about growth. The growth of the body parallels the growth of the spirit if they do what they are intended to do—listen to the God-mind truth and enact it. Therefore, as the body grows, the spirit grows in wisdom. That is the intended way. The team of you, the Brotherhood, the God of the Universe boost you into the partnership with all that is good and bright."

"What about the crucifixion?" I asked.

"This part was the enactment of people's wrong thinking concerning my entity. They thought I came to tear away the old ideas, and they thought I had an alignment with things that cause change. They held to their religious observations and wanted no change.

"Those who loved me were on the brink of despair. 'How could this good man be killed?' they asked. 'Why didn't he call on God to save him?' they wondered. They were not entirely teamed up with my purpose, were they? They wanted me to stay, to fight back, to get the upper hand, to hold the enemy at bay. They wanted a show of strength. They had the show of strength, but they did not realize it. They had the entire truth of God being manifested before them, but they did not open their eyes to it. They did not open their minds, their hearts, their eyes.

"I made the demonstration of enacting the truth in spite of obstacles. I came back in the body; I did everything I could to show them that God is that powerful Teammate Who will see them through to the final enactment, to the body death which means only the resurrection of the real entity, the spirit. But since they could not see the spirit, I had to manifest the body too. That way they could see with their own eyes and believe. But the idea that I came just to prove eternal life is not the point! The point is today and was then that I came to be the one with God that each person can be. I came to heed the truth from God-mind, not earth-mind. This way I entered into partnership with the God of the Universe. This was my purpose."

"Then you did not come to be crucified?" I asked.

"No," came a firm response. "The idea that I came to have people kill me cannot be sensible. I came to enact the truth no matter what problems entered. The idea of enacting the truth is that you will take your own personal and absolute truth and enact it. That may mean standing by it in the face of danger, but that is rare. The truth may require something from you that earth-mind will ridicule you for, but the way to growth is to enact that truth.

"That I faced crucifixion is a fact, not the truth. The fact was that people did not want to have this truth enacted, and therefore, I represented a change in thought, in religion. They wanted no part of this change. Therefore, to enact the truth, I had to accept the crucifixion and enter life again to team up with the entire truth even beyond death. That way I did the teamwork I had to do in order to cling to and enact the entire truth."

I shared this chapter with a friend who had many more questions than I did. She wrote them all out and asked me to seek answers. When I returned to the writing, I said, "You see the questions. However, now that I reread all that you have said, I believe you have answered most of them. Is there, however, anything you might wish to comment on here?"

Calmly, quietly, came the response. "Never think that this entity, this Jesus, will team up with the idea of being the great eternal person who rises on the next plane of life to be above the rest of the entities." Though the message is in third person, it comes from the same Brother of Brothers whom we call Jesus. "The thought of Jesus being the superior being in the next plane of life is a repugnant thought. The entity who was Jesus entered to enact truth. He now wants to help you to enact your truth. That you would believe that either Jesus is God or that he is superior only teams up with earth-mind thought. The entries in the Bible that put Jesus ahead of others add to the enigmatic version of the whole idea of why Jesus came to earth life. But I wish to make the enigmatic plain."

I pointed out that the Brotherhood of God always introduces Jesus as the Brother of Brothers, which indicates a certain standing among them.

Someone other than Jesus replied, "This is only because we here revere this Brother who went to earth life and enacted his truth to become the one who led the way into further God thought. This Brother of ours enacted his truth in earth life, not an easy thing to do, and he now wants to help those in earth life who wish to do the same with their truth."

In Bible study groups, I have heard much about the unforgivable sin mentioned in Matthew 12:32. "And whoever says a word against the Son of man will be forgiven; but whoever speaks against the Holy Spirit will not be forgiven, either in this age or in the age to come." (Revised Standard Version) In the paraphrased "Living Bible," the last phrase reads, "either in this world or the world to come." I asked the Brother of Brothers if there is indeed any unforgivable sin?

"No," came the quick answer. "The Holy Spirit refers to this Brotherhood's work in the open channel where your mind is connected to God-mind. That is the spirit of truth. The 'unforgivable sin' receives its truth from the earth-mind."

I asked about "the second coming" of Jesus.

"There will be the coming of the New Age. This entire period of earth's change will team up with what the God of the Universe plans to reinstate the purity of earth. The teamwork will, however, lead people to new life. The ones who lead, the ones who enter life then to help, they will indeed be the true God-mind persons. There is a thought abroad that Jesus himself will reenter life, but this is not needed." (Jesus speaks of himself in third person.) "Ideas along this line give much to argue over, much to entertain the scholars.

"But the truth continues to enter. It does not wait for Jesus to enter life again. This thought of the second coming is not even pertinent to your life. Therefore, why worry eternally?"

After considering all that Jesus has said here, I asked the value of the New Testament.

"Teaming up with God-mind is the most important way to receive truth. The Bible gives much that was true of that time and place, but unless it impresses your mind to seek your own truth, the Bible enters nothing of value to you. The whole idea of preparing the record is to have a record, right? Those who interpret the Bible to have meaning in present lives are on the right track. But they need to go further. That truth eludes them yet. The Bible may have the clues, but it is not the treasure. The God-mind connection—that is the eternal treasure chest."

I said aloud, "I have no other questions."

"Then write this chapter that I have given you knowing that I enter to be the one to bring the truth of the ages, the truth of what my earth life experience was all about. Present it as I have given it. Then you know that you do what the God-mind truth wants."

CHAPTER 6

BRINGING WHOLENESS INTO YOUR LIFE

After a tramp through a field and wooded area with Peaches, our golden retriever, and Ginger, our terrier, I felt contented and calm. Almost too calm. Though it was only 9 a.m., I had to force myself into alertness, and a mild headache rewarded my efforts.

I put my spirit self into my inner temple, as the Brotherhood had taught me to do, and there I basked in the beauty of this place. Then I thought my body into the temple and floated it in a sparkling blue pool. I spoke to my body, telling it that God-mind is in charge of it, and only the thoughts from that Mind will be allowed there.

I meditated on that scene, fixing it firmly in my thoughts. Then, receptive to those Brothers who counsel me and who help me to receive the material for this book, I placed my fingers on the keys of the word processor.

"Now join the body and the entity that you are." I visualized my spirit self entering my body. "The body is the teammate that will help you to put this writing on paper. This entity that you are enters the body to become the whole perfection. Now rest entirely on the eternal truth that enters you.

"Never think we care not for the whole person which you are. We enter now to do our best work in the perfection of your thought process. This thought process that we want you to enter into teams up with what we teach about demonstration.

"New teammates arrive now, and they bring their thoughts to you. Give them your open mind, and put the entity that you are into a receptive mode. Turn off the eternalization of earth-mind to enable the eternal truth from God-mind to team up with you. Give your best open mind to them now. Ready?"

"Yes," I said. "I'm ready to receive their help." Thereupon, a teammate began to instruct me, but the instruction is not just for me, it is for the readers of this book.

"Give us your entity, your spirit self, to work with here. Your entity wants to fulfill its destiny, its lifetime goal or plan, and therefore, sends the thought into your body to put the inner God-mind thoughts into your brain. These inner thoughts will filter out all that does not pertain to them. In this way the thoughts of your inner being team up with your body to demonstrate the inner being in the outer person.

"Needs that arise will be met when your thoughts turn to God-mind, when they open up to the truth that comes through this open channel. Then the entity which you really are will enter the right thoughts into your brain, and your body will demonstrate the truth of its being.

"Now put the right thoughts into your mind concerning the foremost need of your life."

I asked if this should be a bodily need.

"Team up with the idea that you can become the perfection in your body that you think in your inner self. Team up, here!"

My mind had either wandered or I had doubts about the process. That is why I received the sharp reminder to team up.

"Never allow your body to demonstrate on its own because it is of the earth, not the higher consciousness. It must be subservient to the Mind which is of God. Then your body, which wants its own way very often, will team up with the thought that will give it perfection."

I asked for an example of what they meant.

"Needs of your body may be as simple as wanting to have great health."

Simple, they say?

"This is indeed simple, not the hard thing that people often make it. Team up with us in the matter of health, for example. The body arrives on earth either with wholeness already demonstrated or perhaps needing to be demonstrated. But the hard thing is to make an infirm body whole again. The true teamwork to make this happen must begin with the entity who resides in that body. Babies may be hard to reach unless the parents know this procedure. Doctors concern themselves with the physical, of course, but those surrounding the baby must acknowledge the duality, the entity (spirit) within the body. The baby entity may be reached by teaming up with the thought that the body is responsive to the spirit.

"There is a baby we now choose as an example. This girl baby had no teamwork to help her along the way, for those around her thought she was all physical. Therefore, they tried nothing in the way of reaching her spirit self. They tried this and they tried that physically, but the child did not get better. Then the doctors said, 'You must accept the fact that we can do no more.' The parents cried aloud, and the baby entered into depression because she knew that things were not going well.

"But when the tender ministrations of a person who knew the God truth about our earth bodies teamed up with this infant's spirit self, things began to change. The person gave the baby body with the old spirit the reminder that the spirit within could team with the God of the Universe to bring the body into wholeness.

"Gentle ministrations then appeared within as the soul opened its mind to God-mind. The baby's body lay on the bed seemingly inactive, but within, the spirit began its work of recreating that body. The teamwork started. The body responded. The doctors monitored in amazement. The nurses teamed up to give the baby more attention. The parents turned their hearts toward hope. The body developed, the tender ministrations continued within, and that body responded to the good thoughts that entered the mind of that baby's entity. Therefore, the body became whole.

" 'A great miracle,' the doctors called it. 'We don't know why that body healed,' they told the parents. The spirit/entity within the baby knew why that body healed. The thought, the powerful God-mind true thought, directed the energy of the universe into the areas that needed development, and the creative process teamed up with the body of the baby. There it is—simple!"

Intellectually I understood what the Brotherhood described,

and while I was reading it, the process did seem simple. However, in practice the concept eluded me.

"People who live in earth life for a time must be teamed up with much that enters them through earth-mind," the Brotherhood explained. "Earth-mind does not necessarily give you anything evil, you understand. It intends to give help. However, the well-meaning truth from earth-mind will not team up with the forces of the universe, and therefore, a person only goes half the distance, so to speak. The full power is missing. The wonderful God truth is not there to help the person work out his best destiny."

I asked if it would be proper to do an experiment on ourselves. We all have something or other to work on physically.

"Give your body the eternal truth! Then team up with the God-mind truth as explained in the previous chapter. That is the way to experiment. The healing of a finger, an arm, a foot etc. is only an expression of temporary understanding. The healing of parts is not reality. *Wholeness* is the reality. Your reality thinks *wholeness,* not the healing of a piece of the body as a headache, a burned thumb, an eternal this or that which hampers true body happiness. The best and most powerful thought, and that is what we deal with here, is *wholeness,* and only *wholeness.*

"Let us explain. The body is the whole of something. The thought that goes into this body must also be whole. The thought must encompass the entire body, not the part. What good is the heart without the kidney? What good is the foot without the leg? What good is the nose without the brain? Team up with *wholeness,* not the parts which ache, hurt, get tender, or which withdraw their participation in the whole body. Get into the *wholeness* concept, or else team up with earth-mind, for earth-mind will do you more good than God-mind if you persist in the healing of the parts."

By this time I was determined to get a grasp of *wholeness,* and I asked if it meant every part of the body working properly.

"Team up with the definition that we now give you. *Wholeness* is that which teams up with God-mind. That which teams up with God-mind enters the life demonstration to be perfect even as the God principle means *wholeness.* God is not imperfect, right? Therefore, *wholeness* means no imperfection. As you work with this team of Brothers, you will understand the total concept. Therefore, you need not be concerned in the way wholeness comes about. Your spirit self will think, 'God-mind enters me to bring the truth of my being. This truth enters me to be *wholeness* demonstrated in my body. God-mind truth enters me to be that which completely aligns itself with what is pure, entering into the very fabric of my creative force.' The teamwork we do together, you, the Brotherhood, and the God of the Universe, will team up to be that which enters the healing forces.

"Give the body demonstration in your life. Give the perfection to the world, that perfection which enters to be the God truth in demonstration."

Some people believe they should not take medicine or even go to doctors. "Does this mean," I asked, "that we should rely entirely on God-mind truth?"

"There is teamwork involved in this healing work," the Brotherhood responded, "teamwork by you, the healing masters, the new truth that enters you through God-mind, the truth that people rely on which comes through earth-mind. The healing masters enter your plane from the entry level plane where we now talk to you. These masters refer their truth to the entire body of healing. They want to help people when and if they will be called for. These masters team up with you as we team up with you because they, too, are advanced spirits who use their great talents to help people on the earth plane.

"The doctors who rely on God-mind truth team up with the entire eternalization of truth. They then enter the knowledge into the body of truth that medicine has to give to people. There is much that is of earth-mind, of course, but there is also much that comes through God-mind. But the doctor you choose will be the key to healing methods. If you take the doctor to your inner temple where you think your deepest thoughts, and hold this doctor there to become the one who has your health care in his hands, then you show you want guidance about your choice of a physician. Then if the God of the Universe teams up with this doctor, his face will enter this center of thought again and again in pleasant ways. Then you will know to make this choice. The physician then becomes the earth representative who teams up with you and with God-mind to help you to demonstrate perfect health.

"But when you become proficient in the creative process within your body, and when you put the creative process to work within, then you will make the perfection come about. The physician will then confirm that this has happened. The doctor's job will be maintenance, not healing. This teamwork is part of the true way if people will understand it correctly.

"Therefore, work now with us to enter into the *wholeness* concept which we team up with you to bring. We want you to have this concept within you. There is the perfection that you want, and the *wholeness* concept is the way to have it. That means that you must accept what we say, of course, but the main thing is to put this truth within your being where it will grow into the perfection concept. God wants to give you the best that there is for your lifetime demonstration. Tend to your thinking, tend to your spiritual work, team up with us to achieve the open channel, and the body will enter into the finest perfection that you have ever known."

CHAPTER 7

TEAM UP WITH THE BEST, NOT THE LEAST

This chapter will reach out to grab your mind and cleanse it of all those thoughts of lack, unworthiness and false judgment. Also, the Brotherhood of God teaches us how to tell the difference between earth-mind truth and God-mind truth.

The communicator begins by saying, "Those who team up with truth enter into partnership with the perfect God of the Universe. Those who want perfection as a partner need to understand how to become one with the best truth that comes to them, not the least truth that may cling to them and appear to be valuable.

"Therefore, this message concerns how to know that it is God entering the truth, and not earth-mind. Though earth-mind truth will be appealing, it will not last nor will it give the ultimate in truth. Rest assured there is a difference between these two truths. The teamwork that you, the reader, and we, the Brotherhood, will do together will keep this difference in perspective.

"This is how it is done: Put your God-mind truth into your inner temple, that place within you that you build with pure thought. Here you can meditate and work with your truth. This temple enters your personal being because you build it there, and it reflects that which you believe to be most beautiful and restful. ~~The entire place must be created detail by detail until you could build it in the earth plane if you wanted to.~~ This temple is not without its teamwork, however. The Brotherhood will help you make it the precious temple that you must have within you.

"This writer had trouble building her temple. But we took her step by step into the entire teamwork that finally built it. The temple became beautiful little by little, and she finally realized that she was deserving of this lovely place within her. She had to surmount the feelings within her that she was not worthy of such extravagance. When she teamed up with us to be honest about her feelings, we helped her see the truth of the matter—that the God of the Universe wants her—and you—to have beauty, to have plenty, to have the best in life.

"Until this writer accepted the concept about being worthy of the best, she could not demonstrate the best. She had been satisfied with the least, and why was this? The earth-mind truth taught in churches was that the person who had the least in physical things was the best in spirituality. This concept is erroneous because it belies the riches that the tender mercies of God have to give everyone who seeks.

"Never think that you should not ask for the moon, never think you seek too much from God, never believe that you must become a subjugated person who will rake the dust for crumbs. This is not true. The Father that Jesus presented, the Father nature of the God of the Universe, teamed up with Jesus to help him demonstrate all needs. Jesus wanted to teach the power of demonstration to others, but they were, for the most part, blind and deaf. But they marveled, none the less, about what Jesus did.

"Now put the matter straight. Team up with the Brotherhood to enter into the teamwork of the God of the Universe, the Brotherhood and your own spirit entity. The three of us, this trinity of beings, this wondrous welcoming energy, this perfection of the good that enters to be demonstrated, this projection of the eternal thought—this is what we speak of here.

"Never let your thoughts make earth-mind truth permanent within you, for it is not of God, you see. Therefore, before you become one with any truth, put it into the inner temple you have built. There it will either become crystal clear to you or it will begin to fade. In this way you will know if the truth is from God or from earth-mind.

"Net worth in the earth plane is appraised in terms of dollars and cents. The net worth of this process, however, has unlimited value. It is a matter of concentration, not time, to enter valuable truth into your being. Now work it this way: Think clearly about the truth you think is worthwhile to add to your being. Write it on the wall of your temple, or in some way visualize it there. Then enter the thought of God-mind that you put in charge of the truth-gathering process. This process works by putting the new truth into the utmost clarity if it is right for you, or it will fade away if it is not right for you. This will work. Enter into the process.

"Needs that you have in your life about your work and your relationships develop into permanent thoughts which enter into your consciousness. These needs team up with the inner being also, but there must be a fulfillment of needs, an answered thought that will manifest what is needed. You will meet your expressed needs if you use the process."

I asked what would happen if the needs are not met.

"When your needs are not met, you are entering into poor teamwork that results in no demonstration. The needs are there to be met, not there to stay as they are. The needs *will* be met if you enter into the process described. Needs alert you, but you must take hold of the answer. The needs come into your mind to be met, not to be solidified as they are."

"If we 'solidify' our needs," I asked carefully, "what happens then?"

"If you solidify your needs, you will be the tender truth gone sour. The truth that enters into fulfillment is that which energizes, but the truth that enters into the study of lack and the promise of failure teams up with the law that says, 'No results mean no more truth.' "

I asked for some example of someone in earth life who became one with the best truth, not the least truth.

"Gentle thoughts came to one person to become a teacher of truth. This individual put this thought into his holy of holies—his inner temple. The thought would not eternalize into a clear picture, but he was so sure that such a goal was right that he went ahead with it anyway.

"This person was not pleased with the result at all, though he thought he had used the process we described. He became a teacher of truth, but he did not enter into it with a light and joyful heart. He felt torn between what he was doing and another interest, that of tending gardens. The special interest persisted within him, and he made a beautiful garden, his plan growing and prospering into a business of helping others plan their gardens. The person teamed up with what *he* thought was best, not what was truly best for him."

Another question surfaced. I asked if they meant that teaming up with the best means the best for our own particular entity, not the best in terms of one goal being better than another.

"That is what we mean exactly. Teaming up with the least means that we choose a goal or an idea, or we state some particular thing that we want, without using the perfect process by which we can choose with wisdom. Teaming up with God-mind helps us to know our true spirit selves, our best thoughts, our best plan for our spiritual growth."

I decided that the vocation of teaching truth is not necessarily better than being a professional gardener, and immediately came a commentary.

"The God-mind truth that enters you is the best for you because it produces growth. Your truth is the thing, not concentrating on meeting the needs of mankind. Mankind may need truth, but that does not mean you are the one to go forth to teach it. The truth for you—that is the absolute truth that your soul needs."

"In the beginning of the chapter you said that we want God-mind truth, not earth-mind truth," I stated. "How would becoming a teacher of truth and trying to meet the needs of mankind be considered an earth-mind truth?"

"The noble goal is held up as that which is better than all other goals, but this is earth-mind that teaches such a thing, not God-mind. The truth of the matter is that God-mind pours forth the truth to give each individual whatever is needed to enact the divine plan. Of course thoughts of noble deeds and noble goals may be the truth for some. The person who wants to see the need met may not have the eternal quest to do this thing. Therefore, the truth is the thing, not the noble thought!"

"Spiritually speaking," I asked, "who is the best in this earth life?"

"The person who listens to God-mind truth, enters it into his being and then enacts it in the life experience is the best one spiritually speaking. The least one is that person who teams up with whatever enters his mind to do without using God-mind truth. This person will proceed well for awhile, but eventually he will falter in the teeming thoughts that rise and ebb. These thoughts will seem to open his mind, but in reality these many wandering thoughts will blend into confusion.

"The best spiritual entity will be the one who brings his God truth into the open through the process we describe here. 'The best' does not denote judgment on that soul, but it denotes the way the person enters into God-mind truth in this life experience."

"What I like about all this," I responded, "is that I have no responsibility to anyone except my own spirit. I can choose by way of the truth from God-mind to be and to do whatever is my potential. Am I on the track?"

"Never think," came the answer, "that you must enact any plan other people give you. They only enter into the earth-mind ideas by giving you advice. Listen to the God-mind truth only. Then act. If you enter the truth that appears great to you in the inner temple as we have stated, you will be sure to do whatever your soul is prepared to do.

"The same is true whenever you try to guide others, even your own children. The best thing to do is to put the other person into your inner temple where you will then await the work of God-mind. That person's good may appear or it may not. The person, however dear to you, may fade from the temple indicating that you must not advise this person. That is the way to determine your role in another's life.

"Responsibilities to one another begin in the physical and most end there. The spiritual dimension of the relationships enter the thought process by knowing that God-mind will direct the process. Then you will not make mistakes in this lifetime. The process, you see, is always the same, whatever the big thought, and the work of God-mind within you will make everything clear to you. The person you think you love above all others may face a big decision. The thought within you is to give advice, to do something about this decision. The spiritual dimension, however, is to put the person within your temple and wait to let God-mind direct the process of the relationship. Then the person will team up with his own truth, not yours.

"Now put the thought into your being that you, dear reader, open your eyes to the truth of God-mind operating within your being. The thoughts that stir within you emanate through this perfect Mind into your mind. The thoughts that persist after you enter them into your temple are the ones to work through. They will get you into the perfection of your own lifetime experience."

"Any more?" I asked.

"No," came the answer.

CHAPTER 8

GOD'S TEAMMATE—YOU

In the third chapter, the Brotherhood [*spirit*] dealt with the truth that enters us through God-mind. By accepting the partnership of the Brotherhood, we can make that truth a permanent part of our inner being. When we have made this permanent step of growth, we are ready to become what the Brotherhood calls "the teammate of God." And that is what Chapter 8 is all about.

"This chapter presents the idea that God is your Partner," says the Brotherhood, "not the Big Entity in the heavens who dispenses truth. The partnership is the thing here, not the God-mind which gives you truth."

I could not see the difference between focusing on a partnership with God and focusing on God-mind truth. I asked for an explanation, and the Brotherhood gave it.

"The tremendous truth that enters you through God-mind eternalizes within you as the guiding truth for your life. This truth eternalizes your growth plan, the plan you brought with you to earth, and it helps you to achieve the goals of that plan.

"But the next step you must take, if you are to be one who demonstrates freely, is to team up with the God of the Universe in a partnership. Then you become one with power, for you enjoy the power of your Teammate Who eternalizes your truth with you. You will not be alone in the matter of demonstration, you see. You will be united with the One Who IS.

"Now enter the thought to your spirit self that you are One with God, your Teammate. The oneness is what you must recognize, what you must eternalize, what you must—with your whole being—understand. When you do this, the earth plane is your marketplace, and your God truth is the *eternal gold* you are free to spend.

"The eternal truth (that which is one with your spirit) is what we are interested in telling you about in this chapter. Eternal truth is the only truth for your soul, and you will not find it in the truth books by those who write only their own or others' ideas. Neither will you find it in churches or in the minds of others. The truth that enters you through God-mind is the only truth you must eternalize if you want to become the person you long to be.

"To be that wonderful, creative thought-user, become the one with the open mind, the one with the open heart. Team up with us now to enter into this truth for yourself. Be into the eternalizing of all that God-mind gives you. Never think that God-mind is not the absolute truth. Do not enter into doubt on this, for doubt hurts the perfect understanding which you must have with this pure and absolute truth.

"Now open your eyes to the workings of how the truth enters, why it enters and the eternalizing that must be done. First, throw your old thoughts away. Get rid of old thoughts and open yourself to new ones. Never fear new thinking, for it will prove to be the best you ever had. Put the truth that you will become the person you want to be foremost in your mind. Therefore, the first step is to get rid of old thoughts that offer so little in comparison with your own individual truth.

"Second, trust the Brotherhood who, with Jesus, want only to help you attain your own oneship with God. We work only with the idea that we enter to help, not to get power over you. We care nothing for power, for we in this plane need only to think a thing in order to have it. Therefore, what good would power over you do for us?

"Third, open your mind to the utmost limits of endless thought. That may seem too far for you, but try anyway. Then you will be open to receive the eternal truth that God-mind has for you.

"Fourth, get into the meditative mode to receive this connection. Team up with the Brotherhood who will help you. We stand ready to guide you in this. Be into the meditation now. We send a Brother to you now to enlighten you regarding a wonderful way to meditate. This Brother knows how to reach the perfect meditative state, and he gives this way to you."

MEDITATION

"Concentrate your thought on these words. The perfect thought you want now is that which focuses on teaming up with the Brotherhood. Send your thought to us who enter your force field. We enter to be close to you, to become one with your energy field.

"The body now closes its eyes. It gives itself time to relax, letting each muscle get comfortable. Then the body inhales a deep breath. The breath is let out. This process is repeated until the body enters into the way the breathing happens. Your spirit self watches the process. It watches the breath go in and out. The breath teams up with the thoughts of the Brotherhood. The thought goes forth to us that the body is relaxed and out of the way.

"Now your spirit self enters into our teamwork that wants to help you express the greatness of your being. The Perfection (God-mind) is now entering you. You—the spirit entity—eternalize this feeling by teaming up with those who enter the force field. The Brotherhood is now within the field, right next to you, entering into this eternalizing of the truth that God-mind sends.

"Team up. Team up."

"The connection is thus made. You receive the truth that is tailor made just for you. That is what always happens when this connection is made."

Counseling by those in the Brotherhood helps me sort out my life, to know what is important and what is not. Counseling always leads me to God-mind, to the Source of Universal Wisdom from Whom I receive absolute truth. My concerns are also addressed, and I am led, spiritually, to meet those concerns with truth. There is nothing too small or too big to be met by the truth of God-mind.

The Brotherhood continued. "Individual truth enters to help a person become all that he hopes to be. For example, a person may have a budding idea of some worthwhile goal in life. But perhaps this person hesitates to go out on a limb, so to speak, in attaining that goal. This God-mind connection will enlighten this person about that goal and why the soul has chosen it. That is one kind of truth.

"Other kinds of truth may tell of some of your past lives that have some bearing on this lifetime experience. Or truth may come on the matter of needed medical help. Also, the Brotherhood can help a person expand his consciousness to correct a poor self image or a limited God image. The individual consciousness is that part of the spirit self that reaches forth to enter into the truth of God, but which is hampered by poor or limited concepts."

I asked for some example that might help us understand how individual and absolute truth from God-mind can help us chart our course in this lifetime with greater authority than we have ever had.

"Yes, this is possible," the Brotherhood replied, "The person we think of right now worked to make his lifetime experience all that he dreamed about. He wanted wealth, and he reached his goal in tenfold. This person liked wealth, but wondered if it really should be his eternal teammate. He had doubts.

"This person teamed up with the Brotherhood to learn his own individual truth. What he learned was that he came to earth determined to put money into worthwhile endeavors that would benefit mankind. Therefore, he took his money, which only garnered more money for him, and put it to work. When he teamed up with his Pure Truth, he entered into perfect teamwork that brought him great satisfaction.

"To gain wealth, you see, was only half the goal. When he learned the other half, he attained the open manifestation of the growth plan. This attainment means that he teamed up with God truth and that he grew in spirit in this lifetime.

"The truth of your being comes to you through God, just as our thought here comes to you. There is no way we can use our own thoughts to you in selfish ways. Never fear on that score. We in this Brotherhood have power that extends throughout the universe, but the reason we have it is because we are teamed up with God. The power we have, therefore, must radiate good, not selfish interests, not the portrayed evil that movie makers present about those in the next plane of life.

"We who enter to be your helpers are the Brotherhood of God. We here offer you our help in attaining the God-mind connection to receive your own truth. We want, even more than you can know, to team up with you in this venture. The good thoughts that team up with you will be reflected throughout the universe, readers! The thoughts from God-mind that you demonstrate in the earth plane will be those that will enhance the earth and its position in the great galaxies.

"Therefore, open your minds and open your hearts to the message we bring you in this chapter, the thought that you, the one with God, will manifest your God truth when you team up with your Teammate. Open fully to this message and do not hesitate, do not open yourself to runaway doubts, do not enter into great debate with others over the merits of this concept! Only the forthright eternalization of you teamed up with God will initiate the power that will bring manifestations into the earth plane of those truths that will prove of great benefit not only to you, but to mankind.

"The gentle breath of God is more powerful than the great tornadoes that sweep across the land. The thought that forms a confident partnership with the God of the Universe enters the idea that we can be the powerful beings who team up with the best that the universe produces, does it not? Present those ideas to your inner being, your reality, your spirit self. Then accept the Pure Truth (the Pure Gold) that the God of the Universe invests within your being. The partnership—that is what we emphasize here.

"What more could you want or need than a partnership with God? This partnership enters into the realm of *eternal gold*, the *gold* that you put to work in your earth life, in the marketplace of your physical world. Team up with this Partner, the God of the Universe, the Unlimited One, the Pure Principle, the Host of Hosts, the Greatness Expanded into the Infinity, the Teammate Who eternalizes all that you eternalize.

"This is the end of Chapter 8, but it is the beginning of the whole person, the spirit self with the body self working in partnership with God."

CHAPTER 9

HOW TO REACH YOUR GOALS

"The means to demonstration is not really long and hard, but the truth of your being may make it that way. You know the truth that comes to you through God-mind comes to be your own. And you enter into oneness with this truth because you know its value to your inner being. Not only does it have value to your spirit self, this truth can produce whatever is wanted right there in the earth plane where you live and work. What, then, is there to prevent the perfect demonstration from taking place? What teams up with you to prevent this greatness from happening?"

With these questions, the Brotherhood began to describe and explain another dimension of teamwork.

"We encourage teamwork in perfecting your demonstration to prevent you from entering into discouragement over apparent failure. Many pretend to do what is needed, but they enter into pretenses. They try to convince God they are the 'all-the-way' partners, when in reality they have reservations about the entering goodness of demonstration.

"What happens is this: Your perfect and absolute truth enters your being to be made one with what you experience in life. But this wonderful creative process will not occur until you, in your wisdom and with the help of the teamwork of God and the Brotherhood, hold the thoughts that will energize the truth."

And what are these thoughts? Where do they come from? What do they mean in the process of demonstration? This kind of thought, called here Pure Thought, is the subject of this chapter.

"The open channel brings these Pure Thoughts to each one who seeks them. These thoughts provide the substance that we call the Pure Truth that enters you to become the building blocks to demonstration."

Again and again the Brotherhood states that "There is no work too hard, no tender truth in expression too magnificent, no thought too grand, no tenderness too much to expect when the person teams up with God-mind truth. The tender truth in expression enters as the person with new wealth who can't wait to spend it.

"Those who team up with Pure Thought team up with the best of thought, but those who let these Pure Thoughts pass by to favor earth-mind thought will never know the outward perfect demonstration. Thought from earth-mind weakens the best of God-mind thought. Therefore, the entire message of this chapter is that thought enters people who must either eternalize it or enter into a penetrating teamwork with the Brotherhood. When that happens, we will help each person to distinguish between what is the Pure Thought and what is inferior thought."

Obviously the Brotherhood means that we must not be careless about our thoughts. How easy it is to join in with all sorts of ideas and concepts that bombard us daily! The Brotherhood encourages us to take charge of our thoughts. To be sure we choose only Pure Thoughts, they urge us to enlist their help.

"There is only one reason why Pure Thought enters your minds, and that is to become a permanent fixture. This kind of thought is the eternalization or permanent part of your mind, a part of your inner being.

"Other kinds of thought enter into the communication between our plane and yours, of course. Thought enters into the partnership between you and the Brotherhood. The Pure Thought, however, makes God-mind truth perform the seeming miracle of producing itself in the lifetime experience of each person who understands the concept.

"Truth that we give here enters our temporal teamwork with this writer by the thought process that we use to communicate. Thought, the pure tender gift of God, is the means by which the eternalization of truth takes place within you. Thought is also the means by which you team up with your goals and aspirations. This truth we present may be unclear here, so we will clarify it the best way we know, by giving you examples that put the matter into the focus of you in the earth life.

"People new to truth enthusiastically enter into the concept that eternal truth within a person produces itself in all lifetime experiences. They eternalize this truth quickly, in fact. However, they often get the idea that they must not put the concept to work in the earth plane experience. 'I must not tempt God,' they say. 'This teamwork must stop here, at the idea stage. I must not expect God to help me any further. Now it is all up to me.'

"A person who thinks in this way teams up with divine thought up to a point. Then the thought that this person held in so much value is rejected, and he takes a step backward. Such a person wants to put his truth to work in his life just so far. This individual opens his mind and then snaps it shut when it comes to the final step of thought expressing in his physical life.

"Now turn your mind to this idea: Thought—the process by which we communicate from plane to plane and the method by which we turn the tender truth into the concrete demonstration, is to be understood, not to be given short shrift. That many people stop with the inspiration is evident, but that many people do demonstrate is evident, too. The point to understand here is that truth may *always* be demonstrated. It need not have the 'sometime thing' attached to it, or be a once-in-awhile happening that may or may not enter your life.

"Teamwork is the answer to the problem of demonstration. It is the key to perfect demonstration. Take the example of the woman who ended her life because she did not meet her expectations in her career. This woman, teamed up with her truth, gave it her best eternalization, and then she stopped short of putting her truth into expression. She teamed up with the earth-mind idea that it is only a matter of luck as to whether or not goals can be met. The truth was in her, the bright and enlightened truth that her goal was to be met, but she then withdrew to a position of a beggar in the temple. There she was, her beggar's outlook reducing her mind to distorted truth, thus giving truth the short shrift.

"Truth we speak of here is the collection of Pure Thoughts that a person receives through God-mind. There is also a collection of thoughts that enter from earth-mind, and these thoughts often add up in a person's mind as the best there is, when, in fact, they are only trivial truths.

"Give your bright and shiny truth the eternalization to your being. Hold it there (by means of Pure Thought) until you become one with it, but do not let any other truth hold on to you. The truth from God-mind is just that, perfect and absolute. Therefore, do not get the earth-mind truth into that act. The entry of earth-mind truth (also through thought) will contaminate what you have carefully put into your being. It will enter decay, pollution, putrid false premises that people generally accept just because people have always accepted them.

"There you see two kinds of thought, Pure Thought and plain restive thought. The Pure Thought is the kind miracles are built of, but the restive thought is the kind that turns God-mind truth upside down and backwards.

"Team up with this Brotherhood to get rid of the falseness that tries to enter your being. We will help you to ascertain which truth is the one to polish and to bring into manifestation. Team up, you who read this chapter. Team up, those of you who read but scoff. Team up, those of you who give your intellectual powers to this book but not your open mind! Team up! The God of the Universe longs to have you express your truth in the physical world, in the marketplace of life. Give yourself to this task which will make your lifetime experience rich and teamed up with noble goals.

"Be the one to demonstrate truth, not the one who relies on self. Team up with the Brotherhood in this matter. Hold our gentle truth within, but give it only to those whom you know to be the true entities who honor the work of this Brotherhood.

"Better truth than we give here will not be found. This truth holds you to the real point of our entire communication—the point that the teamwork that we do here places us on a one-to-one level, not a one-to-class level. All this enters to bring us wisdom, not foolishness. This truth enters to hold us to the gentle expression of God-mind, not the expression of that which is not of God. Therefore, hold yourself in the situation here.

"Now let us temple (join together) the truth of what we say here with an example. There are those who want to express God truth, but who hold the idea that God will not enter into their individual goals. With this thought, these persons wipe the wisdom of the ages from their beings. The weak thought they apply to their situation belies the truth that God is the only power in the universe. People who want power, who want good in their lives and who enter into the wisdom of the ages, work with the Brotherhood to bring God's truth into expression.

"Teaming up with each one of the attributes of God results in that attribute working through you into an outer expression of your life. Now do you see the importance of this total work? Entering into just the eternalization is good. It is needed, but it is not enough yet. The final step is the demonstration itself. Give yourself over to this truth. Team up with total eternal truth which demonstrates into expression as those beautiful goals you have in mind.

"Pure Thought—that which is your working material, your substance, your best tool in working through the lifetime experiences—is matter, not vague nothingness that many people think of. Thought is the eternalization of the truth that you take for your being. Therefore, control your thoughts. Center them in the God of the Universe who encompasses all the good that enters to be used. This thought that comes through God-mind, this thought that is the eternalization of truth, this thought which is the Pure Substance that brings the truth into manifestation, is what we bring to your attention now. Team up with the understanding here. Give it your total concentration. Tender your own thought to your inner being that all thought is matter, and therefore, you choose *only* thought that has the touch of God in it, the touch of eternal wisdom, the touch of truth.

"Nothing in your earth plane will ever come in to hurt you when your thought enters to offset it. This means that you control your world if you enter into the concept we bring you here. These thoughts that you may have taken lightly for your entire lifetime eternalize within you to enter into manifestation. But you can rid yourself of the earth-mind thoughts if you remember to heed only God-mind thought. The thought is what you give energy to, you understand, not just the truth of God-mind or the truth of earth-mind. This truth falls around you, but what you enter into yourself is what you give thought to. Then you wrap it in energy, in your own good pure God energy.

"Thought is hard to express in earth life terms, for earth life is concerned with physical things that they call 'concrete.' But the *real concrete is thought,* for it is thought that molds each person into what he really is. Therefore, the word 'thought' is far from the tender idea that wafts in the air. It is, instead, the heavy concrete that dries into forms that cannot be altered.

"Weaving the words that explain this process is the work of thought, it is true. But this thought is intended to be the expression of the thought form of ideas and of concepts. This kind of thought is the beginning of what is known as the 'thought-gone-templing' because it tries to create within the being pictures or paintings or feelings.

"Tender thoughts, that is, thoughts that have not yet been cast in concrete, give a person pictures to work with, but yet they are not in their final form. As we exchange ideas, these thoughts are what we use, for the most part. Each individual wants to belong to one or another truth. The vacuum within the spirit must be filled with truth of some kind; therefore, you must be alert to put the best truth within your being. This best truth that comes through God-mind will present thoughts to your mind, thoughts that you must consider. Then, what you do next determines the value of God-mind truth in your life. This is how it works. Do you understand?

"Belong to the wonderful thoughts that will eternalize within you as you give them your energy. Belong to these thoughts with your open mind, your eternalization, your teamwork. Give yourself over to total understanding so you may make your demonstrations over and over, not once in a while.

"Now work on these thoughts we present here. Work on God-mind truth. Remember the truth that thought is matter, not the wafting of ether, not the wafting of non-energetic communication. Thought is the certainty of matter, the substance of the universe, the pure and unrestricted gift from God."

CHAPTER 10

PRINCIPLES OF GOOD DEMONSTRATION

"We are now going to teach the principles by which you may use thought effectively to make your outer demonstration. We also will help you to make your own demonstration by leading you step by step to a successful outcome."

We were getting down to practical applications, so I was eager to receive this chapter. Although enthusiastic about spending my *eternal gold* in the marketplace of my life, I had no idea of the problems that hampered my own demonstration of truth until the Brotherhood continued.

"Truth that pours tenderly into you through God-mind teams up with your spirit selves. The ones who read this book, and the one who writes it also, will not enter into anything here that will throw them into discouragement. God-mind truth never fails you, for the teamwork that you have with God-mind and the Brotherhood of God eternalize only that truth which is yours. Therefore, do not let any thought of fear negate what we give you in this chapter.

"Put your inner being into the energy of your inner temple where you work with thought. The temple may be built within you by thought, by the visualization that becomes the reality of your being. This temple opens you to basic spiritual work that prepares the way for demonstration.

"This temple is one of the gifts that must be taken advantage of here. If you have no such inner place, now is the time to build it. Make the temple a place of beauty that teams up with your being. There is no model for this temple. It need not be like pictures of temples on earth. It need not follow architectural tendencies. This temple is for you only, and therefore, it must be your own personal thought of beauty, of wonder, of eternal comfort.

"This temple encompasses your being. Team up with it. Take time to create a wonderful place within you where you can be tenderly ministered to if need be. Here you can be taught, you can open your mind to the newness of thought, and you may invite the Brotherhood to work with you. Teammates from the Brotherhood will enter only if you invite them, but a door must be made there, a door which you may open from within.

"Truth that we have will not team up with you until you open those doors. This means that the counseling, the communication that the Brotherhood does, will not enter this private temple unless you want it to come. Therefore, open your temple to let us help you through this perfect demonstration. The Brotherhood never enters to hurt, never enters to make fun of you, never enters to give you wrong thoughts. We have only tenderness for your being. We operate by the Tenderness Principle. Therefore, rest on this principle.

"Never make yourself eternalize thoughts that you do not perfectly agree with. The demonstration will not work properly if you try this. This particular truth, even though it is wonderful, may not be what you want just now. Therefore, enter into partnership with the truth you believe to be right. This principle involves your spiritual readiness, your eternalizing of the truth to which you have opened yourself. This is known as the Consciousness Principle. When you have the temple within you, we will work with you on your own consciousness raising."

The dictionary defines consciousness as "the totality of one's thoughts and impressions, the mind." I asked the Brotherhood how they define this word.

"The word 'consciousness' as used here is that which a person believes and holds true in his or her life. Raising your consciousness is a matter of rising to higher thoughts, higher vibrations, higher teamwork in your work with God-mind truth.

"Raising the consciousness involves the work of the spirit self, the mind, with the entities who enter your being. These entities come only at your invitation to work with the raising of your consciousness. That is the work of our highest Brothers, those who specialize in helping in the work of the inner being. Giving yourself over to their ministrations enables you to move swiftly in the direction of making your individual consciousness team up with what is highest and best. This is how the principle works within you, but remember, it works only at your initiation.

"Now that we have discussed the principle, we move next to the 'how' of making this work in your daily lives. What use is there of working with truth in the spirit unless you can make the bodily application? That is why you are here in this body, is it not, to make a partnership with the mind and the body, with the spirit and the world around you? The process of the life purpose is the truth first, then the body. We call this process the Truth Before Material Principle.

"Your physical needs may overwhelm you. For example, many people team up with the entire picture of happiness when they try to make a demonstration. This is not the way, however. Take out any picture that tries to make a partnership with everlasting happiness. It cannot be well defined, and therefore, cannot materialize. You must put it into exact detail. This is an inviolate law or principle, also. The principle is explained in this way: First, the truth that you want to demonstrate must be placed in your mind in picture form. It must be well defined, very carefully detailed.

"Therefore, 'happiness' is not a thing to try to define clearly, is it? We call this principle the Truth in Energy because it must team up with the God energy that knows exactly what this truth is.

"Wonderful results come to one who enters truth in detailed form. This result will eternalize first in the mind and then in the outer or physical world. That is the absolute rule here, the rule that works in this plane and which works in your plane also when you put the principles to work."

The explanation up to this point seemed clear enough to me,

so I asked why so many people fail to demonstrate what they say they really want in life?

"There is no reason why many people cannot demonstrate what they say they want in their lives. But the matter rests entirely with them. The word that we give is the truth, the way things really are in spirit. But there are many who wrap themselves in a physical response to all things. The entities which you are, the readers of this book and the writer, too, must give your old thoughts partnership with the wind that blows through your mind to keep it clean of the earth-mind truth. Then you can apply the steps according to our prescription. The steps are indeed clear. Why not prove them for yourself?"

Perhaps, I thought, it's a case of what to demonstrate first. A thought crept in that I'd better begin with something simple. Then, I wondered what I should do if I fail in this? Does failure mean that the system doesn't work? Or does it mean I'm inadequate to the job? Questions, questions, questions!

"Questions only tend to enter doubt," came the reply. "Then doubt holds a flame to the whole truth, and it goes up in smoke. These questions only serve the earth-mind kind of thought. The truth wants action, not questions."

In spite of everything, I still had reservations about proving God-mind truth. It was almost a case of paralysis. If I do nothing, I said to myself, the expectation will always stay that I *could* demonstrate this truth if I wanted to. But if I try and fail, then I have nothing to fall back on. I asked if this made any sense to those who give this step-by-step process.

"This proves only that you think that God-mind truth will not enter the marketplace. The point of working through this process is to prove to you, and there is nothing wrong with proving something, that the God-mind truth is exactly what we say it is, perfect, absolute, and worthy to spend in the marketplace of life."

I confess that I read and reread the above material many times before I could move ahead. I left the word processor and got a cup of coffee. Never before in the receiving of truth had I felt so "on the line" with what must come next. Could I, would I, be able to move off dead center in this matter of demonstration? spirit

Finally, I confronted my own thoughts. The Brotherhood of

God has always told me to be honest, first with myself, with God, and also with them. The very fact of this communication is a demonstration, of course. This has been the most positive lifetime influence that I have ever known. The truth that I have become one with has helped me enormously in my relationships with others, no small thing. My health has improved since I have received this counseling and guidance. This must be a demonstration too, right? Then what more must I do? I asked for the truth from God-mind to enlighten me.

"The truth you seek here must team up within you before you can use it, of course. This truth speaks to your very core, to the inner place where you keep your secret thoughts and doubts. The eternalization that took place before you knew of the God-mind truth made its bed within the temple of your being. This truth says to you not to try to make God perform tricks. It says to you that God is too great to be used in any way that favors self. This truth you have become one with generates no action because it projects a thought of God, the Almighty One up in the heavens someplace, who is concerned only with the big issues of life. As a result, when you want help, you beg for His attention. And when a perfect answer is given, you promise, even swear, not to bother Him again! You have made eternalizations that force this valueless thought onto your being, and it is this worthlessness you are trying to spend in the marketplace of your life.

"This 'worthless money' will not work in your plane or in this plane either. This Teammate that you want to communicate with is not the One you hold in your inner being. Put them together as One Person, One Principle, One in Perfection. When you have the God concept within you that holds this God to be what He really is, you will demonstrate."

So there it was, not a very good picture of my inner self, divided and unable to hold the true focus on the God of the Universe. I knew from other books we wrote together that there was no way to move forward in spiritual development until a person develops this larger view of God as universal, as principle, as total power, as perfection. Frankly, I thought I had tossed out that old truth about a judgmental God, a God that frowns down at me and Who has outrageous expectations. I honestly did not know, until God-mind truth enlightened me, that I still held what I consider archaic views of God.

When God-mind gives you the truth about yourself, you recognize it immediately as ABSOLUTE. Therefore, I examined my view of God whose truth will pour out to anyone who wants it, whose gifts will appear for anyone who reaches out for them. Obviously, I had not married this vision of the great God of the Universe with my inner being, the core of my spirit self. Nor had I told my body (brain) that it must now respond to this new view of God.

I asked the Brotherhood if they knew of this duality of the God concept within me. They replied, "The duality you speak of is not the point. The point is that you have only entered part of the truth to your inner being, not the whole truth. This is what we see here."

My thoughts formed definite intentions. I do not want any notion within me of a limited God because obviously such a notion is false. Therefore, I focus on the universal concept, the great power in the universe who is there for everyone whether or not a person forms a confident partnership with Him. This great God enters me and anyone else when we open our minds to this greatness. I asked the Brotherhood if I was on the right track here.

"This is indeed the right track. The truth that you now focus on will team up within you and tenderly take it to your inner being. The old concept, the one you see clearly for what it is—false—teams up with the wind that blows through your temple to clear away the false thoughts that you push out of your being. The wind carries them out the window of your temple into the far reaches of the universe where God makes them into new universal energy which will have positive, rather than negative impact."

Normally the Brotherhood believes it is unwise to share personal truth with others, but here they think it might be helpful. I visualized that old truth falling out of my being and tumbling around within my temple where a strong wind carried it out one of the open windows I built to overlook a lovely view. This visualization, the Brotherhood tells me, helps me to understand how the spirit operates. I asked if this better God concept is part of the consciousness principle.

"This is indeed part of raising your consciousness. This process enters now to improve your God concept, but do not think the process is now over, for understanding the great God of the Universe will be with you always."

I indicated I was now ready to move forward with this chapter and with the demonstration which I must do. "The ~~Broth~~ _spirit-_ erhood wants to commend you. Opening your mind to the truth of your being is what you have needed to go forward. Therefore, now you are, at least, on the track. There will be much more growing to do, you understand, but you have opened yourself to the next step in your personal development.

"The demonstration now may move forward. Teamwork that we do here together opens you to make a demonstration that will prove this process we now lay before you. This is the process: The first thing you will do is to enter what you want very badly into the energy that is eternally present in the universe. ①
This energy is that which God has to give you when you understand how to use it."

I paused to let these words form their perfect meaning within me. What I want was easy enough. The eternalizing of the energy took a little longer. I decided to give this energy some kind of dimension that I could hold in my mind. Finally, I compared this energy to the radio and television waves that go through the atmosphere to the cable from which we get our signal.

All I have to do is to focus on this special golden cable that shines and pulsates somewhat with the energy of the atmosphere. When I want to direct this tremendous energy, I simply turn it on by twisting a knob that opens the circuit. There it is, the energy of the universe entering my pictured desire. A transformation takes place. My pictured desire vibrates with the universal energy, and unable to remain only a thought form, it springs forth into physical form.

"This process works well for the writer," the ~~Broth~~erhood S commented, "but the reader may have another way to picture the eternalized energy going into the pictured desire. This perfection which must be demonstrated enters into the perfection of what is of God. The process is now complete. Where is the thing you want? Eternalize this one more time. The thing you now seek is there in the physical form if you will but reach out for it. This thing, this wonderful desire in physical form, is now materialized. Team up in this matter.

"If you have not entered it with positive force, return again to your workshop, your temple, where you will once again team up with the energy that enters the proposed desire. Then repeat the steps. When this is complete, team up with the God of the Universe. Now put your focus on this great God, the One whom you cannot even imagine no matter how great your concept is. God knows how the process works, you see, for this Presence enters the process too. This is the method you can use to put your truth into the marketplace as *eternal gold.* Tenderly thank this Father God that the process works, whether or not you see this thing you want. Thank Him because this again reinforces your own belief system.

"Now put this whole process to bed, so to speak. The process works, but when it involves other people, the tender truth must also work through them. Remember, if the thing you picture teams up with others, if it requires their open minds, then the process will work to overcome their resistance, perhaps, or to enter them into the project. But yet the process works."

I am one of those who asked for something that involves other people, so perhaps the above explanation was for me. To have the demonstration the way I want it, many other people are involved, and the finished product calls for cooperation from them. Therefore, I asked what else I might demonstrate—a stone or a coin or something like this?

"The demonstration works best when you enter something you REALLY WANT. Making a demonstration just to have something you do not want is a very weak process indeed. Therefore, stick to what you want VERY MUCH. Perhaps you want a certain home, or a pretty girlfriend or a special job. Then you must enter this in specifics. The demonstration works if you can be specific. Clarity and details—the big MUST of success."

I decided to try another demonstration, leaving the first one to work in the universal energy to get the cooperation of the other people involved. There was a more concrete subject at hand, and I decided to visualize it. However, I had certain misgivings. Could any desire be called "crass" or "unacceptable"?

"The crassness you team up with is only crass if you declare it so. The unacceptable desire would only come about when you want to hurt or otherwise bring harm to someone else. The request will open itself to demonstration only if it works for the good of you or of others, not ever the other way around."

I again visualized what I wanted. The visualization was concrete. I added details. "Team up with the visualization that will clarify this request," the Brotherhood said. "Specify the good that this desired thing will do. Give this concrete subject a push into the universal energy which turns it into concrete. This entity which you are in reality (your spirit self) will team up with all the greatness of the God of the Universe to bring this concrete thought into manifestation.

"Enter into the perfection that you eternalize within you. Team up with the manifestation, with the confidence you now feel about this matter, with the tenderness that works through you and from you to others. Give God the thanks because it is *His* principle which makes the manifestation enter your physical presence. Get into the flow of energy and hold it there.

"Teaming up with the Brotherhood will enter you into the realm of the eternal good masters who work with these principles to make demonstrations. This procedure is the perfection that works in the marketplace of life. Get into this flow of energy. Use thought to make use of this truth, thought of the process of how this demonstration is made.

"Thought must be controlled, entered into God-mind, held in the flow of energy. Perhaps you work at this and still nothing happens. You look around you and say, 'Hey, nothing happens!' Work patiently with your thoughts for awhile until the thing is perfected. The entity who you are must be patient because it takes much practice for some to be masters who demonstrate rapidly. But it will come! This is our promise.

"Give this work daily exercise. Team up with us to perfect your power of thought, your power to visualize, your power to link the thought of the desired thing with the God energy. The demonstration will manifest; it will become physical because it must enter into expression. There is no choice here. This works!

"Now we rest our case to let you, the reader and the writer, team up with all we have given in this chapter. Become one with this process, one with the principles involved. When you master the principles, the demonstration will appear. Be patient until you become proficient. Then team up with us to go on with the rest of the book."

With this review, the Brotherhood ended the chapter on teaching and demonstration. No one who reads this chapter will be more in need of review than I was at this point. No one who tries to demonstrate and then perhaps feels either foolish or disappointed will need more practice than I needed. But it is here I remembered how slowly the communication began that I now undertake with such ease. Practice. Yes, that is how I learned to write the communication that comes from God-mind with the help of the Brotherhood of God. And it is with practice that I will learn to demonstrate the powerful God-mind truth that I have within me.

CHAPTER 11

GOD—THE BRINGER OF GIFTS

The night before I received this chapter, I had a vivid dream about tornadoes. Some of these started high in the sky and descended to earth in narrow fingers that curled somewhat when they touched the earth. Others came from clouds near the earth, and these tornadoes appeared squat and dumpy. I watched them closely, but with no particular fear. Remember, this was a dream. Moving fast, an unusually large whirlwind of black dust came directly toward me. I glanced behind me at something or someone with whom I identified, and then faced the tornado. "This is it," I said to myself. "This is my tornado." Even then I felt no fear. I merely marveled at its size.

I asked my Counselor what this dream meant. "The tornadoes were the truths that you have been studying. They entered your being with various kinds of reactions, and the size and shape of the tornadoes represent your own feelings toward them. The biggest tornado, however, represents the biggest truth—biggest from the standpoint of your own individual spirit. This is the truth you marvel at, the truth to which you feel attracted. You glanced behind you because you were checking on your needs. This big truth ahead of you would meet the needs you were protecting, if you would but give them up to this truth."

Chapter 11 reaches into your heart, your mind, your entire being. You are being challenged, even as I am, not only to become one with your truth from God-mind, but to demonstrate it in your life. Once more the Brotherhood allows us to focus on the principles that lead us to spend our truth in the marketplace of life.

"This wonderful and great God of the Universe enters to give you His gifts of spirit. These gifts enter the eternalization process through the partnership you create with them. The partnership will depend on the truth you team up with, of course. This chapter will present the understanding of what God IS, what He wants of you, and what you might want of Him.

"The great God of the Universe teams up with those who open their minds to Him. But He who is the Principle, the Perfection, the Wholeness that we often speak of, will not force Himself upon anyone. This understanding must be the elementary thing to receive into your minds, that God never thrusts Himself upon you.

"Now make right whatever holds you back from entering into partnership with God. Make right the misconception that is the result of earth-mind thought. The eternalization of earth-mind thought results in seeking more and more of this thought, always looking for that which satisfies your being, but of course, never finding it. Yes, that is the way your mind will go—reaching toward the goal of understanding what God is, but never attaining it until you get rid of the earth-mind truth.

"The goal of your heart, and the goal of every heart, is the same. You want to be one with the God of the Universe, for you were created to be the One or Son of God. There is no way you can get rid of this goal, no more than you can change the human body into the animal form. The goal is permanent within you. That is why everyone who hides the goal from his consciousness will team up with whatever presents itself as worthwhile, trying desperately to fill the yearning of the heart for what can only be filled by the greatness of God.

"Now put the eternalizing that you have already done while reading this book to a test. First, send the thought to your mind that your spirit wants to be One with this great God of the Universe. Now let your mind feel the effects of this great thought. Hold it there until the thought is firm. Now you are ready for the rest of the truth test.

"Put each truth that you want permanently on top of this great thought of Oneness. What happens to this truth? Does it waver? Does it become even more clear? This overlay allows you to test the truth of your being to be sure that it IS the truth that God-mind wants for you.

"Now you are ready to enter this truth that you are sure of, the truth that eternalizes into an even greater firmness within your mind. This truth is yours forever, and it wants to be demonstrated! Team up with the Brotherhood and let us help you manifest your truth. Each must do this as an individual. Your truth is not necessarily the same truth that enters another. Therefore, we must deal with you on a person to person basis.

"Now pay attention to this next thought on the matter of the great God of the Universe. This God, this eternalized One who abides within the universe, opens His truth to all of you who want it, no matter how evil you think you have been. God enters to give. He never enters to judge, in spite of what the ministers preach.

"Ministers present the misconception of God judging us harshly in order to give us the assurance of salvation. But only God enters with the entire picture of our souls, not ministers who rant and rave about the evil in men's hearts, about the wrong they see in the world. They only reinforce the wrong, the evil, the energy of these awful deeds. They give these negative eternalizations a temple to work in. The truth stands on its own, without churches, without ministers. The truth that enters this energy you have access to pours forth without any thought of judgment. Therefore, reach out without fear, without guilt, without any thought of restraint.

"God, the Wonderful, the Great, the Perfection. What else in your life could give you the teamwork that He gives? What else could give you the tremendous assurance that God enters to give? Here we stand, this Brotherhood of God, to present to your understanding the God of the Universe, but there are, among you readers, those who back away. The gentle truth enters, but many turn away.

"Right now we eternalize the truth that enters those readers who reach out for it. We promise help from our Brotherhood.

This teamwork is our plan for helping you with your lifetime experience so you will not waste your life.

"Now, put yourself into your inner temple where the warmth of the light of God holds you in constant gentle presence. This warmth, this light, enters to teach you how God works with you. Eternalized truth abounds within the temple because the spirit is open. That is how it must be to gain progress in growth. Then the spirit teaches the body how it must respond and how it must conduct itself. The mind surpasses the brain in authority. This means that the individual truth is what you must seek out if you are to put the body in order.

"Never write off the Greatness aspect of God. The word is bandied about, but the tender truth that 'God is Great' seldom enters its rightful proportions. God, the Universal Being, is more than Entity, more than Principle, more than Perfection, more than the Eternal Truth in expression. This Great God of the Universe enters your own open mind, your open heart, your open eyes, your open ears, your temple where you team up with Him. Get into this picture we give you of this Greatness, this Perfection, this Goodness in expression, this energy that makes thoughts become the things of the physical world. Now, work with us to become ready to open your mind to whatever aspects of this God that you can put in your inner being. This is the way to enlarge your God concept even further than you have done before.

"Your needs will then be met because this concept brings power, the power of God that extends through you to the world. This is how God puts forth His truth into the eternalization of the worldly plane.

"Tenderness that God sends resides within you to bring you into the true tone of those whom you want in your life. God tenderness works like an attracting force to bring those who want this tenderness they feel in you. This great God brings all His gifts to you. Therefore, wrap them in Pure Truth, the Pure Truth that God has entered these gifts to your use.

"If nothing happens when you use the eternalization process, then team up with us in the Brotherhood to learn why. The eternalization may not work because you will not enter the God-mind truth as absolute. Therefore, you may turn away from it even though you feel attracted to it. The God of the Universe prepares your truth so that you will enter into the demonstration of it with great passion, not great reluctance. That way the energy goes forth within you to the energy of God, and the inevitable happens—God performs His truth within the temple of your being which in turn takes it to the marketplace of your life.

"This understanding of demonstration is fully explained through this writer who even now is working with this truth. She wants to manifest certain things in her life, and she works with the principles, with her purpose, with the teaming of her energy with God energy. This way the manifestation is now ready to be shown her, to be put into physical form."

Even as this truth poured through me to the word processor screen, I stopped to respond to the doorbell, and I signed for a box and an envelope. Both are from the publisher who wants to make our first manuscript into a book. The tangible evidence of a contract, along with other truth books he has published, constitute the first step toward my desire of seeing these books in print.

"This writer teams up with us to promote the publishing of these books. They will enter into the marketplace as she has determined they will—paperback, inexpensive, good printing. They will team up with those of you who now quit the worthless, aimless transactions with what you think must be God. These books team up with those who reach out for the best gifts they could ever have, the gifts that God brings to each of you.

"Teaming up with the God of the Universe is what we enter into these books by the truth-giver, Jean K. Foster. This entity who teams up with us came to her body to team up with us, to write these books, but this is another story, a most interesting story.

"Now put forth your spiritual hand to us who reach toward you with great tenderness. The beings here who wait for your hand want to lead you through this wonderful process of enacting truth. This is the reason why we work with this writer. This is why God establishes this Brotherhood to be your true Brothers, your true Communicators.

"Needs that work within the minds of the readers reach us, but these needs must not be eternalized within you. The needs themselves will not bring you the good that you want. The needs only open to more needs, right? Therefore, put the energy of the universe to work on your behalf by opening yourself to the entities who help answer these needs. They want to help you to meet these needs by working with your own perfect truth. This truth is what you must tune into here, not the needs themselves. Tenderness abounds here in this process, so do not think you must push yourself. Bask in our tenderness.

"When you have this tenderness established between us, think of what you want to enter your life to provide you with what you want, desire or dream of. This wonderful thought must team up with our good thought which blends with yours. This way we help you to strengthen the manifestation. Tenderly we enter the thought, then tenderly connect you to God-mind. There the truth pours through you to tell you how to deal with what you desire. This truth enters to give you the Way, the True Gift from God."

CHAPTER 12

OPEN TO THE PRESENCE OF GOD

My husband and I climbed to the large overlook which jutted out into Waimea Canyon on Kauai, one of the Hawaiian islands. Filmy clouds in various shades of gray spun slowly around the peaks while other moist spirals explored the red and green ridges that ran down the mountains. The sun side of the volcanic ridges was starkly revealed, but the other side was deeply etched in dark shadow. As we watched, the earth turned, and the sun opened every crevice in its powerful gaze.

When we finally turned away and directed our thoughts toward our next destination, I felt sad that all I could take away was a memory and a few pictures.

In this chapter the Brotherhood leads us into a spiritual experience which compares with the visit to Waimea Canyon, with one great exception. We need not go away from this experience with only memories to sustain us.

Pure Truth, the subject of this chapter, precedes the truth of everything else, including our individual truth. It expresses as the God of the Universe. Therefore, put away your needs, your goals, all the desires you have been working with. Become still and open yourselves to the Brotherhood who leads us in this beautiful, awesome experience of being in the presence of the God of the Universe.

"Needs that you have been attaching to the demonstration of truth are to be put aside. Team up with the Brotherhood in the temple of your being, this temple where you work with truth. By this time, the eternalization of the most perfect temple surely must team up with you easily. But if you have not taken time to perfect this temple, do so now.

"The temple eternally teams up with what is lovely and perfect. Turn your creative thought toward its beauty, its tremendous quiet energy that pervades the entire place. The openness of it, for it must not be confining, should let you expand, move about and eternalize more and more lovely things within it.

"Now put yourself into this temple. Eternalize its great beauty within you. We enter, too, to help you to perfect the details. We add gleaming gold to that wall! Isn't that a fine touch? We add a bit of alabaster to the gentle curve of that trail into the far reaches of the temple. And here lie the gems. Throw them upon the walls to add their gleaming depth to the gentle feel of great eternal power. There! The whole place teams up with what the God of the Universe wants to give you.

"The entity which you really are, the spirit self, enters into the thought of your temple opening to God Himself. Not through the doors you built for us to enter, mind you, but it opens up to that which is beyond your present thought. Give us the way to present this thought of Pure Truth to you. Open the temple. Now team up to receive the Pure Truth."

At this instruction, I visualized the top of my temple melting away, but the sides were still intact.

"The eternalizing process of your spirit turns now to the God of the Universe, the Power, the Principle, the Perfection, the Entire Truth that exists. Now open your being, open your temple, let it open its whole top to this One who enters to be One with you. Needs fade away. The Pure Truth remains. The teeming thoughts tenderly team up with us to give their attention to this Pure Truth. Now eternalize this thought of the God of the Universe waiting only for the temple to fade into nothingness around you. What need is there of this temple when God is eternalized?"

My temple melted to the ground level around me and I, my spirit self, stood there expectant and unafraid.

"This beautiful thought crystallizes into the entry of the One whom you want to be with, the One you open yourself to completely. This process overwhelms the entire thought projection—you. Now give yourself over to this Goodness, this Truth in Action, this Being which enters tenderly to team up with you. The temple, though lovely, opens to the beauty beyond thought, beyond every expression. This being, this God of the Universe, presents Himself to you, entity of the earth form, because He enters Himself into your teamwork to become One with you.

"Do not put this thought aside. Team it up with your own good entity who wants to be one with God. This thought entity, this human part of you, this getter of great eternal truth, pushes to become that which it was intended to be—the entering expression of God here in the earth plane. This earth form knows it is of earth, but it yearns to express the Perfection, the Positive Force of the God of the Universe. Go to the entity now, give to him or her the understanding that God, the One Who enters to be One with the spirit form, will offer His open truth to those bodies who serve the spirits.

"Your needs do not return yet, however. This great God must complete His special visit with your spirit self. The Great God and the Eternalized God within the human form, join together now to become One. Give this Pure Truth to your body—that God is present to give His message to it. Enter this thought to your body now. We wait."

I read the above material again and again. I am spirit/body—one in the sense of my spirit connecting with God-mind to receive the Pure Truth, and my body is Truth in expression. My oneness comes from the power of the God of the Universe Who works through my spirit into my body to produce what is called the "thought-form" or body. "This entity who enters to be the spirit/body is now the teamed up partner of the God of the Universe," the Brotherhood explains.

"Here is a message of Pure Truth: *Gentleness that overcomes the evil things in the world now passes through you.* Team up with this understanding. This Pure Truth overshadows needs, goals and the overpowering truth you have held previously.

"Your spirit/body wants this message, for it has feared the evil that it believes is in the world. This fear, this thought form of evil, entered the world to team up with eternalizations of what passes as the truth from earth-mind—thoughts of mistrust, hopelessness and teeming miseries. But now this order of things is reversed. The gentleness that overcomes the evil things in the world now passes through you. This Pure Truth overcomes the fearful thoughts of evil in expression. Then the world moves toward the better expression. Team up with this great Pure Truth.

"Give your spirit/body another Pure Truth: *The God of the Universe establishes His kingdom in the being with whom He speaks.* The truth of this promise enters the spirit/body to find that great happiness overshadows this person even though he stands in the God presence without his temple. Nothing teams up with the Spirit/body better than this message of the Kingdom of God. What the spirit enters, the body reflects, and the body now fairly dances with joy. What better truth to hold in the mind than this one?

"Now enter the third Pure Truth: *Those who eternalize their relationship with God never turn their gentle thoughts to earth-mind again.* No one will ever be the entity which he once was, you see. There is no way to face God in this way and then turn your back on Him. Team up with this great truth in order to put your lifetime experience into thought waves with God. The tone of your being adjusts. The vibration changes. The gentle truth of the Pure Truth permeates your being, spirit and body too. This truth rises to the pinnacle of what enters as Tenderness, Perfection and other thought projections you enter from here on out."

I struck the question mark key several times. "Teamed up thought projections?"

"Thought projections become the realities in your life. They emanate from this experience of standing in God's presence receiving these Pure Truths.

"You now receive the Pure Truth that enters to you, through you, to be part of you. This Pure Truth is the result of experiencing perfect teamwork between you and the God of the Universe. Team up with this chapter the best that you can to enable you to go forward into that which you want most, the complete demonstration, that which gives you the practical entry into this plane that will allow you complete freedom of movement.

"Team up! The God of the Universe intends you to have open eternalization at your command, but there are many who think of this concept as impossible. Therefore, meet this great God, bask in His presence, open yourself to His Pure Truth. Then you will end the separation between your plane and this and enter here when you wish.

"Team up now to rest your mind which has stood in this Presence, this Perfection, this Absolute Goodness, the Trustworthiness Beyond Belief, the One with the Eternal Greatness. Rebuild the temple. The temple now houses the God of the Universe, and there will be this great difference between the temple that *was* and the temple that *is.* This temple eternalizes perfectly whatever is genuinely perfect for your being. Therefore, the true power teams up with these good desires to manifest. That is our special message, our special truth message in the midst of this book on getting your own truth into demonstration."

CHAPTER 13

THE WEARER OF TRUTH—JESUS

"Turn your thought to the one who teams up with you, to the Brother of Brothers, the wonderful Counselor, Truth-giver, Gentle Entity, Giver of His Tenderness. Your thought must go out to this one who comes to describe the best relationship that you can have with the God of the Universe. This one presents the true picture—the tender, gentle growth and the whole teamwork that takes place when God and man or woman give truth their mutual partnership.

"Never think God withholds His partnership. His greatness extends to you openly, in every matter, on every thought, entering you at your invitation. But the partnership will not be able to take place until you, the reader of this chapter, will enter into the agreement. A partnership exists only when all parties agree."

The Brother who introduced this chapter then said, "Here is the Master Teacher, Jesus." With no further preliminaries, the Master began.

"Needs that enter my mind from your mind allow me to hear your pleas for help. But whenever these needs express in this way through the ether, they enter unattended. Let me explain. People toss forth their cries for this or that. They cry out their thoughts to the heavens. The ether forms the thought so that we in this plane often *see* as well as *hear* the needs. But they open us to sorrow. Why? With the rudimentary understanding that is given in this book, you can meet your own needs on your plane. The God of the Universe enters into partnership with you if you request this to take place. The thought goes forth to God, and there it is! The thought expresses into the physical through the power of the great God of the Universe.

"Therefore, work to become a good partner, not one who is articulate at expressing needs! Needs only express lack. A partnership with God expresses the substantial gain you can make by tuning into every great gift He has for you. Give yourself the *opportunity treatment* here. This treatment *expects the opportunity to eternalize, the opportunity to be your great potential. The *opportunity treatment* expects prosperity that derives from the great Source of all creative power. The *opportunity treatment* enters with wonder and great expectation every day.

"Open to the entity which I AM, please. The 'I AM' that I speak is not the name 'Jesus.' The 'I AM' is what every entity belongs to in the way of truth. Therefore, the 'I AM' is whatever I have put into my spirit self that is Pure Truth, as well as that which is my Individual Truth. What I say about me is the same for you, the reader. What you are in reality, the 'I AM' of you, is whatever truth that you have entered permanently into your being.

"Tender truth, remember, is the recognition only, not the oneness. Therefore, only *reading* truth, only *saying* that it is eternalized does not mean it is permanently within you. The entered truth is that which belongs to you because you have made it operate in your earth life. Every person must put his truth to work or it will not stay within your being.

"Now enter this tender truth to your list of truths:

The God of the Universe wants to be your partner in this lifetime experience. This truth may seem old, it may seem trite, it may seem to you that it is nothing new at all. But how many do you think put this truth to work in their lives? The number is not enough, believe me. Enter into this wonderful truth because the partnership with God eternalizes within you only when you want it and when you use it."

Why, I wondered, would anyone refuse a partnership with the powerful God of the Universe?

"Thoughts that enter here go like this: 'The God of the Universe? Well, if I could believe in Him, maybe I could be that partner.' Or another says, 'The Truth? Well, that is hard to swallow. The truth is what my eyes, my ears, my other senses tell me.' There are some who say, 'God is not the powerful One, or why would He allow tragedies to happen?'

"Then there are a few who tell themselves that there is no God at all. These persons place value on earth alone, and enter into earth truth without eternalizing the values of the spirit. Therefore, their life experience becomes that of an eternal quest—an endless search for truth without ever finding satisfaction.

"When you entered into earth life, you knew there was this great God, and you wanted to get His truth installed into the experience you would have in that plane. But some of you did not put truth into your spirit with enough resolve, and it fell by the wayside. Then there are others, who promised industriously before they went to earth, that they would hold to the truth of the spirit, the truth that recognizes the great God of the Universe. They entered earth life with a certain eternalization in their minds, the thought-form that insists there is a God, there is the divine element in life. These people often hold to their truth furiously, but they omit the main consideration, which is to put their truth into their life's experience.

"Everyone must demonstrate, you see. Demonstration is putting the truth on the line to give the pure energy of the God of the Universe to the earth plane, to enrich that plane and to add to the wealth—not to deplete it. Needs that people have are to be met with their permanent truth. Therefore, the eternalizations in the earth plane only come about because people bring them into being through the process we present in this book. *Spirit*

"Team up with the Brotherhood, my good brothers *companions* who enter your plane as the advanced spirits that they are to help you with the living of your life. These advanced spirits enter to be my arms, my hands, my mouth. They work with me. They will enter the earth plane as I enter it, open to the God of the Universe, energized by the Power, the Presence, and the Energy that teams up to everyone who wants it.

"Great eternalizations will be possible for you to manage when you put the partnership into your life. This greatness is not for God alone. Nor is it for me only. This greatness is what God holds out to His partners, those who team up with Him.

"Tenderness goes forth from me to you. Various thoughts that you become aware of are there because I send them. The thought transference works to bring us energy that will team us up with God. The partnership that I, Jesus the Christ, have with this great God comes about because He enters willingly and because I enter willingly. That is why we work well together. This partnership, however, is not just for me and the Father, as the Bible quotes. This entity that I AM, this thought-form of God's, is he who is one with God.

"But I come now to assure you once more that it is not only I, but you, that the Father awaits to include into a partnership. The partnership is for you, and you, and you over there in the corner waiting to see if others can do it. This partnership is for you, however timid you are.

"Peering through the eternal ether at you, I see you entering into this partnership that will open your minds, open your hearts, open your greatness. The God of the Universe tenderly teams up with the entity that you are.

"Gentle thoughts surround you now. Put the truth of your being within you. Enter the Pure Truth that we gave in Chapter 12, and then enter into the truth which combines with your being. When the partnership exists, the entity which you are is ready to demonstrate.

"Be open now. Enter into this partnership. Get into the flow of these ideas. Put your 'I AM' into this eternalization that God is already one with you. There is every expectation here, every gentle thought giving you its message. The partnership is established. The entity that you are, the great 'I AM,' wants you to hold this truth before the teammate which is God. Now put this partnership on paper, like a contract. Sign it. The God of the Universe may enter His name or He may not, but His presence overpowers you, holds you, energizes you. Step forth in abundance!

"Eternally the question arises, who is the Teammate, this God of the Universe? Where is He? Why team up with Him at all? All these questions enter to find answers, to learn why we ask them, to begin our personal search. God, with whom we enter into partnership, gives us our very personal truth, truth that teaches us who we really are, why we are here in this lifetime experience and why we want certain goals to be met, thus eternalizing the truth of our beings. This eternalizing that God helps us attain is that which the Teammate (God) wants entered into earth thought in order to improve it. Be the one who understands! God wants the God-mind truth to abound.

"Never hold God to be just an entity who sits on a throne. A throne would not hold all that is of God. That returning thought dies, waiting for the answer that will never come. One person notes, 'Teeming thoughts about God quiet my worries over earth needs.' Yes, the many thoughts of God, however gentle, enter to satisfy your questions. Give yourselves the tremendous good news that God enters not as man, not as I or these Brothers, not as the person we might want to know. God enters to be the *temple itself*, the temple of your being.

"God enters as the temple because He is that temple. The thought projection which built that temple within your mind would not eternalize the thought of God because God is so much more than anyone might eternalize. That is why we here keep telling you there to enlarge your temple, to make it grandiose. The temple represents your present concept of God, the Teammate with whom you work to learn truth and to give truth to others.

"Now enter into this temple with your eyes open to see the beauty, to see the enlarged version of it, to hear the sounds that you put there. This is the temple which is God Himself. This is where you work with truth, where you enter into meditation, where you want more truth.

"Be the partner, the perfect partner, and empty out all your old thought about Him. This temple will teach you, will bring you secrets, energy, great gifts. Therefore, team up!"

Here the transmission from Jesus ended, and the one who began the chapter took over to conclude it.

"The Gentle Entity has told you how to be a partner with this great God of the Universe. This one wants you to hold this entire truth in your own consciousness until the temple fairly leaps to become larger, more beautiful, more powerful. The truth we bring you in this chapter has ended now, and it is ready to be perfectly combined with your own perfection."

CHAPTER 14

GETTING THE TEAMWORK INTO MOTION

"The teamwork we speak of here is that which exists between the Brotherhood, you and the God of the Universe. 'This
is fine,' you may say, 'but how am I to get this teamwork un-
derway? How do I begin? Where is the starting point?'

"The procedure begins with you. Your teamwork cannot be
passive, nor can it begin unless the prime mover wants things
to move. No, God is *not* the *prime mover.* God is the Pure
Truth, the Wonderful Teammate, but He is not the *prime
mover.* 'Why?' you ask. 'Isn't God all powerful?'

"The tenderness of God is only part of His nature. His tenderness allows you to be free to act however you want, free to
enter into partnership with Him or not. The God of the Universe teams up with you only when you activate the relationship because He wants you to open your mind, open your
heart, and open your truth center."

One of my old tapes played its familiar story in my brain. It
went like this: "Here I am in this human body, and there is
God somewhere in the heavens. If He loves me so much, if He
is indeed my heavenly Father, why doesn't He help me without
a lot of fuss?" Immediately the truth entered its response.

"The God of the Universe is not the Big Entity in the Sky!
This wonderful God Principle IS the quality we speak of. He IS

the Gift and the Giver. God is there to be used, not to use. This tremendous wonderful Teammate is the Pure Substance we use to make our thought projections. God is so vast, so tremendous that you cannot hope to enter into a perfect understanding of Him."

I suggested that perhaps we should omit pronouns to indicate God. The word "He" makes us think of a large, powerful man in the sky. "She" used in reference to God, though enlarging the concept somewhat, still makes us think of a person.

"There is the fallacy," the Brotherhood returned. "This great God is the True Being in the sense that Goodness, Greatness, Purity, Awesomeness—the entire scope of creativity—is this One. But God is not Being in the sense that you think of now. The being that is you now holds God within, but the being of God is expressed through you, not held in Its entirety within you. Jesus demonstrated God by eternalizing the God self which demonstrated perfect truth within him. Therefore, God expressed through Jesus.

"But God expresses through you and you, and you, too, remember. The Being which is God is only *part* of God, not the whole God self. Therefore, when we say 'He' or 'She' in relation to God, we mean that God works with each person, that He enters into our lives, that He enters His Pure Truth to our understanding.

"Teamwork gets things started in your life and gives you eagerness to be on your way. The way we work together is with the universal energy which now flows through you. New tender truth pours into your mind through the God-mind connection, and gentle presences enter to help you operate with abounding energy. The eternalizations on the matter of truth give you permanent bonding with them, and this process opens the door wide.

"Now energy presses upon your mental process. The truth enters into thought-forms, whatever the entity wishes to make visible in his or her life. In this way the eternalizations enter only to be pushed out into the visible world. This is our plan. Team up to open yourself to this thought process.

"The eternalizations that we bring forth, the thought-forms that you now hold in your temple, team up with the useful energy of the universe. Think this through, and you will see how this is done. We, the Brotherhood, work with you by way of these gentle presences who enter to help. They understand how to bring about the proliferation of God in the universe. They know this entity—you—and want you to perfect your gifts that God has for you.

"New thoughts that enter you through the God-mind connection interest you. They are the truth that you seek to live your life by. This truth settles the perturbing tendencies to follow too many trails of thought both from earth-mind and God-mind. Truth from God-mind helps in making choices, trying to decide how to enter whichever truth seems best at the moment. Yes, the God-mind connection enters true thoughts, and these will enlighten you in the living of your life. But there is more.

"Gains that you make into the best truth open you to the entire presence of God. These gains are those manifestations that you want to come about in your life. They combine exactly with the truth you now live your life by.

"Therefore, push out the thought forms that base themselves in your great God-mind truth. Team them up with the Power, the Presence, the Greatness which God is. Then the prime mover, you, turn your truth into the perfection of the God plan."

I reread the above material, and I wondered why we were writing an entire book about demonstration when the process is actually very simple to explain. As usual, the explanation came quickly.

"People's needs often take precedence over any other thought. They bury themselves in their needs, their desires or their goals. Then the truth escapes them entirely. This is why we must go step by step, very simply, tendering our teamwork ever so little, inching along until the reader suddenly cries out in recognition, 'Hey! I know what you mean now. There it is, the manifestation. How simple!'

"First, we must get your attention. Second, we give you the truth about this working relationship. Third, we help you to enlarge your concept of God. Fourth, we enter to work with you, step by step, becoming part of whatever it is that you need in order to have complete understanding." spirit

No doubt I am a good example of why the Brotherhood must work slowly, step by step. The Brotherhood has had my attention for over a year. From the beginning of our communication, they gave me counsel and helped me make the connection into God-mind. I worked to become one with God truth—again and again. As for my concept of God—it has exploded (in slow motion) into a vast new creation. Finally, I see the demonstrations taking place in my life. Therefore, isn't it ludicrous that I, of all people, would ask why we write an entire book on the subject?

The Brotherhood resumed. "This writer teams up with us daily to enter into our counseling. Teaming up is now easy for her, but the work had to be done—the work of practice, attention to detail, the art of meditation, practicing the presence of God-mind. No doubt the entity who writes this book eternalizes our teamwork in order to have it, but the being she is enters into our good counsel in order to stay centered and to be her best as a thought receiver.

"Nothing arrests the pace of the demonstration like unattended teamwork. The entity who pays no thought to the teamwork process will not realize the manifestation that he holds in mind, and here is why. No entity works by himself or herself in the earth plane. Deceptive in its enticements, the earth plane eternalizes the practice of working together with other earth beings. It does not eternalize the need for work within their spirits to get truth through the great God of the Universe. Therefore, people join together in order to achieve the interim projects, but they seldom think togetherness will take them through the entire lifetime experience.

"The teamwork we advocate is not only for the short term, but it is for the total lifetime experience to its completion, to the crossing over to this home plane. All of this means that spirit has lasting values. Spirit has the totality of a person's life in the mind of God. It is not concerned with only the short term project.

"Gentle presences, part of the Brotherhood, enter into teamwork whenever they are called. "But who can predict what earthly partners will do? Will they be there for you in every condition? Will they stretch forth their hands to give eternal wisdom and the potential of tenderness that your being cries for? Will earth friends remember to unite as one with your needs? Will they band together with you to bring fulfillment to your every desire? Earth beings, the ones cloaked in flesh, team up with you to bring themselves, their thoughts, their hopes and dreams, yes. They hear yours, too, but there is no sure teaming up, is there?

"The entire teamwork that you do in the earth plane is to benefit more than one person, right? The teamwork you do with this Brotherhood and with God is only to benefit you. You must realize that this is *not* a self-centered goal. Those who want to reach their goals and desires are not reaching forth with selfishness. The entity you are wants only to be one with the eternal plan for his or her soul. That is the quest—to be one with the growth plan, with the God-self. They enter as the same, the growth plan and the God self. These represent that part of your nature that joins itself with God, whether you recognize it or not.

"Team up, therefore, with the Perfection which is the God of the Universe. This One enters now to be your Greatness, your Entire Thought in Action. Open your mind, open your heart, open your being to the entry of those who rush now to help you become the entity who manifests truth."

CHAPTER 15

THINKING: THE PROCESS OF BECOMING

"The teamwork we do together—the reader, the ~~Brotherhood~~ *spirit* and the God of the Universe—explains the process by which we all grow. You, the Brothers, everyone! The eternal thought process—the way we direct thoughts within our minds—tells our body selves how to behave. The process also tells our spirit selves how to team up with every thought that will assist it in becoming one with God.

"The matter of learning how to control the process is what we concentrate on here. Otherwise, the reader may not truly enter into partnership with the process. Give your being its rightful information, its truth, and then know how to direct it within the thought process. That is the way we work if we are to get into the flow of great truth.

"Teaming up with the God of the Universe is the way we enter thoughts into our minds, of course. The great God of the Universe gives His truth to us whenever we tune in and ask for this truth. God enters into our being only by invitation. We discussed this matter before, of course. But we emphasize it here because there are many who eternalize God, and they don't know how to receive His great truth. They believe that all they need do is to become still, perhaps. Or they enter into what they call 'communion' with God. Perhaps they meditate. But the right way to get truth eludes them altogether!

"The eternalization of God—thoughts that present a picture of God—is not the way. The eternalizations only prove one thing—you do not have a big enough concept of God if you think you can eternalize Him! Therefore, do not even try to eternalize the God of the Universe.

"The way to be His truth receiver is, first, be open minded. This means do not turn away the many truth thoughts that come from God. Team up with what these thoughts tell you. Never think God leads you astray!

"Second, enter the thoughts into your holy of holies, your inner temple where you work with truth. In an earlier chapter we entered this temple into the process of working with God. The temple within you, remember, now holds some part of God, and He is the nourishment that this temple feeds upon.

"Third, act upon the truth. The eternalization that you want to be teamed up with is that which flows out through your own truth, not the truth others perceive to be true. Nor is your truth that which comes from the ideas of a person you might admire, or from the perfection that you hope to be but do not understand. Throw away these old ways of processing thoughts! Turn instead to the way we give you here. Be conscious of what you do here. Team up with the entire process to be one who demonstrates the absolute truth of your being.

"Give your being the greatest gift it can be given, the thought process by which it becomes one with God! This entire message, simple in its words, is open to all, open to your understanding, open to your achievement. The only way you could fail is to enter into the entire plan without your own indestructible and entirely perfect truth.

"Gentle presences surround you while you work this over in your mind. Tell your brain to be silent, to be submissive to your mind, which is spirit. Your brain is a reflector, not your master. Tell it where it belongs in the order of the universe. Tell it to withdraw while your mind works with truth. When you need your brain, you will call it forth. That is the way your mind must operate if it is to take control of your body!

"Gentle presences—yes, they tenderly approach you now. They only want to help you enter into the thought process by which you become one with God. They want you to give your

Spirit

teamwork to the Brotherhood and the God of the Universe. They have no selfish motive. They greet you, entering into your temple if you want them there. They tenderly explain the process as we have explained it in language. They explain it again to your mind, over and over, as many times as you need to have it repeated. They stay to help, to sustain your being throughout this entire thought process. Give them your attention, your understanding of why they enter.

"Be the perfect partner who will open your being. Give these gentle presences your best gift—your expressed tenderness towards their presence. Your expressed needs focus their attention on whatever it is that holds you to the body, and they give their attention to these needs to give their blessing or to intercede on their behalf. But their focus is to turn your attention to the eternalization of your temple, their presence, and taking hold of this wonderful thought process.

"Awaken your inner being to the necessity of holding this private pattern of thought. Eternalize the process working within you. Then take it for the wonderful message that it is, the pathway to the tremendous proof of the existence of the God truth within you. Team up with what we say here. Team up with us to have complete oneness with this thought process. Send your own thoughts to the eternalizations that have been explained here. Then the entire process will be clear to you, and it will be open to your understanding. This entering truth will change your lifetime experience into one that is publicly centered in God without words being spoken, without explanations being given to others, without credence being accorded to those who may think the God of the Universe is making a fool of you.

"Be into this new thought process, and stand every thought on its head that is not focused in the way we have explained. Give this new process sway over your being. Then the miracles happen."

CHAPTER 16

THE CONFIDENT PARTNERSHIP

"Teaming up with the God of the Universe eternalizes much that was not open to you before you made your commitment. The truth that God is able to pour out to you will never turn you to wrong temptations. This wonderful God gives only what is good for your soul. Never allow the thought to remain within you that this great God leads you to situations that will bring terrible suffering upon you. What would be the purpose of such heart-wrenching eternalizations? God wants only the good, for He is that Good. Therefore, He is incapable of teaming up with anything that is not pure, that is not tender, that is not the kind of truth that satisfies.

"Give your open mind to this partnership you have entered into. Team up your thoughts with those that God enters to help you. Present the Great Entity's Being into your own that you may express His innate Self by opening your own being to the thoughts He sends.

"Announce your new partnership with God to your body self by thought and by word. To give truth its stationary place within you, use your power of thought correctly. Arrest the God message right there within your wonderful being.

"Gentle thoughts try to bring the best emotions to each truth. That is the way they enter into truth, by teaming up with their best emotion. These gentle thoughts enter to change your very soul, you know. Yes, they change your soul to one of eternal blessing, to eternal generosity, to each considerate act, to each eternalized gift of truth made manifest.

"Gentle thoughts abound when you become the partner of the God of the Universe. These thoughts are not temporary; they are permanent. People will marvel at the gentle nature you have. They will enter your eternalization to try to 'catch' that same gentleness. Then you must remind them that they, too, can have this gentleness they admire. The tenderness which comes through the open channel by way of God-mind teams up with those who have avowed their partnership with God.

"Enter this thought: *Team up with the God of the Universe not only to receive truth but to be the partner in a steady relationship that brings total fruition of your great goals.* Give this matter serious consideration. Team up with that which is exactly what it seems to be.

"Gentle thoughts will bring you understanding of others, bring you the gentler outlook upon those who seem to do 'wrong.' These thoughts will give better voice to the expression of gentleness. New thoughts enter regularly now—gentle ones, yes, and also those that come to solve problems. The thoughts arise from within the temple where God has been entered. They push their way up through the temple and wave at you for attention. These thoughts must be heeded.

"Much truth that we give you here opens your mind to what God is. This writer works with truth when she walks, when she is at rest, whenever she has time to wait for something, time she might otherwise waste. She also works with truth at her word processor. The truth she receives is that which is only for her spirit self, the truth that will help her to become her potential.

"She pushes this truth into the workplace of her soul, and there she teams up with it. Enter into this work easily, you who read this book. Enter with joy, with tender appreciation. Then the truth slides in easily. It does not clash with anything previously entered there. Gentleness is like the lubricating oil that opens the valves and makes the machine work smoothly.

"Now pay attention to what we next give you. Tender truth, that which is not yet part of your being, sometimes eternalizes in your temple, but it stays there inactive where you can look at it from time to time. The only way to put that entire truth within you permanently is to initiate the energy that must bring it to the forefront of your mind. That area is where you put the truth you expect to live by. It is here in the forefront of your mind that you work out your entire life plan.

"Be open. Eternalize that which you believe in, that which you hold only in your temple. Put it out in the open where it will act in your life. When you leave it within your temple, the truth is like a jewel that you put in a safe because you are loathe to wear it in public lest someone steal it. What good does the jewel do you? It is only in the safe. That is the way it is with truth when you leave it in your temple. This truth is not working for you out in the marketplace.

"Great energy flows to you who has become the partner of God. Enter this energy in your life experience, and use it openly. This energy proliferates—like all else from God—when you use it. Therefore, spend the energy on that which is of value. Team it up with all that is eternalized. Then your life will take on the activity which is God expressing in your life.

"Now put the entire thought process in the 'oven' of your mind, the place where things happen. That 'oven' gently works with whatever you want it to. The truth, the partnership, your initiation of the work of this team—all this enters the truth into manifestation.

"Every person who enters into partnership with God also enters into every possible good. This happens because the God of the Universe persistently gives His good to His partners. Wait! Make this truth permanent before you go one step further, before you go even one page further: God is what He IS, Good, Eternally the Giver and the Gift, the Teammate Who enters the great good that He IS to His partner—you!

"This great thought eternalized, or made permanent within you, teams up with all the energy that the universe expresses. Then this energy enters into your plans, your best ideas, your good goals, your oneness with tender truth made permanent within you. Team up with the Brotherhood if you eternalize anything less than this greatness, and we will help you to extend the truth to encompass all that will bring new power into your life.

"Become a child here, a child who wakes up in the morning

awaiting the excitement of the day. This child knows no thought of doubt or of poor truth, for he is always open to the greatest truth known, the God-mind truth. 'Why is this?' you may ask. When these children turn their unimpaired thoughts to Him, He teams up to bring them the entire truth of His Being. He enters into their plans, their goals, their eternalizations.

"The God of the Universe brings what is joyous to the child. Send the thought to your inner temple that you are the child in essence when thinking of God and all the potential that He is and that you are too. Then your life will become full of great wonder and will become one with all that brings you into your good growth pattern. Give your open mind to this message. Nothing eternalizes unless a person opens his mind, remember.

"The truth will lie dormant within your temple unless it bears the fruit of your oneness with it. This means that you must—*must*—demonstrate the truth of God within you or else that truth is entered within you for nought. Team up to enter into this message with your open mind, then.

"Now eternalize this thought before the thought evaporates: *Truth is yours to use, not merely to look at.* Never think inspiration is enough. The inspiration is the father to the act. That is the way with God-mind truth. The truth of earth-mind, however, often enters only to inspire. Therefore, this kind of truth will eventually let you down as you try to work with just inspiration as your guide. What you need is substance, and the God-mind truth is entered into you as substance, that which will eternalize and which will express in your life.

"Gentle presences surround those of you who have straying thoughts, you who want the Greatness of God but stand fearful and hesitant. These presences extend their spirits to your spirits, giving you their eternalization to make use of. Their truth is strong within them, you see, and they will let you lean on it. This is known by many as the everlasting arms of God—the warm presences who enter the spirit presence to lend their strong resources. Eternalize these who enter to help you as you read this book, as you contemplate the action required. That way, your mind knows them, recognizes their presence and their teamwork with you.

"Now, enter into our great message given in this chapter. Turn your mind inside out. Team up with the Partner Who will enter you into the halls of the Great. The teammate that you are and the Teammate that He is now work together with the authority that brings what is needed to express truth.

"Never think of what was before this moment. Never let your mind become distracted to other thoughts of getting power. There is only One Power. Now put all this within you. Enter into the Eternal Entity which is the God of the Universe. The entry completed, you now have the 'confident partnership' which will team you up with the tenderness that abounds, the tenderness which gives you the perfect entry into the hearts of mankind.

"Nothing enters to hurt you—ever. Nothing enters to bring you unhappy rewards. The truth is all that enters, the truth that your own soul reaches out for in order to become one with God.

"Team up. Team up. Team up."

CHAPTER 17

KEY TO A SUCCESSFUL PARTNERSHIP

My husband and I stood with a small group of people waiting for dinner to be served in a nearby dining room. One man told a story of his trials and tribulations in fixing a washing machine. He took the back off, and the pegs that regulated the timer fell out. He tried various combinations to put them in correctly, but each time his decision proved wrong. That night, he said, he had a dream which gave the pattern for inserting those pegs. In the morning he did exactly as his dream indicated, and the timer worked perfectly.

"Now, don't look at me strangely," he laughed. "I didn't say God gave me that dream or anything. I can't explain it, though."

"Why couldn't it have been God?" I asked, thinking how easy it is to tune in to the Divine Intelligence which is God-mind.

"Yes, why not?" His tone held a note of defiance.

Thereupon another person, new to our community, told her story. The parents of a school friend of her son took him to their house to play. She was to get her son in two hours. When the time was up, she realized she didn't have their address. To make matters worse, there was no telephone listing of that name. She needed the name of a person she had met who would know how to locate the people, but she could not remember that name.

She went upstairs to her bedroom and lay down on her bed. In a very few minutes the name came to her mind. She also said she couldn't explain it.

"Could you do that any time in order to solve problems?" I asked. Immediately she agreed she not only could, but had done so many times before.

Two days later, the following material came to me through God-mind with the help of the Brotherhood of God.

"Needs that arise in your life often take over your thoughts. Needs try to absorb the mind, you see, and then a person will turn not to God-mind, but to earth-mind. Why? Because needs often overwhelm those in the earth plane.

"Panic enters to give a person great eternalizations of disasters. The thought of meeting these needs is wiped out by these disaster thoughts. But when people turn quietly to their inner being, the spirit itself, and then turn this spirit to the open channel to God-mind, needs will be met. The needs in themselves are never what they seem to be. They give people the opportunity to prove their truth, to put it to work in the marketplace of their lives.

"An individual who trusts in the God-mind receives better truth than the individual who quickly turns out of habit to earth-mind. Needs often cause people to think in terms of poverty which explodes within them as the awful truth that has come into their lives. The poverty we mean here is not necessarily money, though it could be. It is also the poverty of spirit that believes in the great disaster, the terrible catastrophic illness, the teachings that say they receive the punishment of God or announce that there must be terrible happenings in a life that has heretofore had great good.

"No one who wants to meet his own needs teams up with the earth-mind truth. Those who team up with that inferior truth only want to find company in their misery. They want others to sympathize, to give them solicitude. They cry out and others join them in their cries, but there is no forward thrust in meeting their needs.

"Some may say, 'Get even with those who wrong you.' Others may say, 'It all will pass,' and some will recite the old saying, 'You must take the bitter with the sweet.' But none of this inferior truth satisfies, does it? That same truth may even go so far as to tell you that God sends problems to you so that you will progress spiritually. Well, they are only half right. God never sends anything negative upon any individual. But you do grow spiritually when you reach out in trust with your Partner, God, and meet those problems.

"Great entities who enter the earth plane to demonstrate this work team up with God and they do demonstrate over and over again. But the entities without trust write such demonstrations off with a shrug and the words, 'Some people have all the luck,' or some such statement.

"The truth that will eliminate worry, concern and everlasting eternalizations of wrong thoughts teams up with those who reach out in confident trust to their Partner, the God of the Universe. This is a Partner who will not fail you—ever. This Partner has been accepted by you, and He will never desert you. The nature of this great unlimited God is not petulance. Nor is it one of jealousy. God's nature is not eternal vindictiveness toward real or imagined sinners. Rather, the nature of God is Pure Good, Pure Understanding, Pure Tenderness, Pure Truth that is just for your being.

"The person who presents his or her needs to God-mind teams up with the Partner, the entire Being of what God IS. Even though the individual may not perceive the open-ended concept of God, trust is the key to having needs met. The greatness that is God is not put off by small needs. The examples the writer gave at the beginning of the chapter are the kinds of things not considered vital to life, yet they are the needs of a life experience which must be met.

"What we learn from meeting what might be called 'small needs,' is that the Greatness of God meets all needs, not just those that indicate life and death. Team up with the Brotherhood. Learn to turn over every little worry to this Partner who enters your life to make it an open tribute to His Perfection. Tenderness that God gives you abounds. Open your mind to this tenderness. The Greatness that is God teams up with you, the object of His tenderness. Therefore, every concern of yours is His concern. Every thought for help that you send out has a response. Why not? Why would the Partner help you with some needs and not with others?

"It is you who enter limiting ideas about what God will or

will not do. Gentle thoughts that enter you to allay your fears come from God-mind. Thoughts that enter you to become impressions that lead to good action enter you through God-mind. Tenderness abounds, and you on the earth plane, who need to put your truth to work in your lives, can solve all problems with trust in your Partner, the God of the Universe.

"Now put your mind into a neutral mode. Those of you who have already begun to communicate well may have your own key to meditation given you by the Brotherhood through God-mind. Therefore, turn to this key. Give it your attention.

"If you have not yet begun to communicate clearly, turn your mind to some neutral place where you feel happy, comfortable, safe. Team up with this scene and let no other thought enter while you examine each detail of this lovely spot in nature. Hold this picture while your mind comes to a point tenderly giving your Partner your trust. Get into the scene. The God of the Universe, this vast God whom you cannot totally hold in your mind, offers His energy to you. This creative energy teams up with you. Hold this picture.

"The creative energy flows over you. The time is right to enter your first need. What should you do about this need? What insight will open your mind to creative solutions? Team up with this creative energy again and again while you present your needs. The Brotherhood helps you. They call out to you, 'Team up with the Brotherhood. Enter into our good help that you may receive your own truth through God-mind.' The thought enters and persists. This is God-mind truth. *spirit*

"Never think we turn away from you. Not so. The Brotherhood always stands ready to help you to complete the connection. There may be tender moments when the God-mind truth overwhelms you with its clarity. There may be times when the truth enters and teams up with you to the point of unbelievable joy! This truth holds nothing back, you see. The truth spills out, its beauty teaming up with your soul and leading you in the true paths of righteousness.

"No one will ever be teamed up with half-truths or hurtful truth. Believe. Team up. Team up again. Then trust. Now the truth of this great Mind is yours.

"Give us your hand, reader of truth. Give us your minds, open and willing to expand. Then team up with the hopes and the dreams of the person you really are, the truth that you have permanently made yours. Team up with all that presents itself to your true self. Get complete oneness with this message, for then you will have great satisfaction which the partnership with the God of the Universe can produce."

CHAPTER 18

UNION WITH GOD—A PERSPECTIVE

"The truth that surpasses the perfect union with God has not been discovered. Pure Truth teams up with what God IS, not what some tell you God says. The *nature* of God is the important thing to consider, not the many words that tell of God. Therefore, put yourself into union with the God of the Universe to enter into the eternalizations which will create all that you want in your lifetime experience.

"The entity which you are, the spirit self of you, eternalizes what is wanted of life. Dreams, goals and all manner of good thoughts fill your head when inspiration runs high. But unless there is union with God, none of these wonderful thoughts turn into the reality of materiality. Team up with what God IS, what He has to give you, what the Greatness, Wonder and Perfection bring into your life. The thoughts you extend to your Partner, God, become His concern. Therefore, team up with Him in the union of spirit.

"God is your Partner. This has been well established by now. The partnership enters its crucial phase here, however. Unless you do more than give the partnership your blessing, nothing will really come of it. The wonderful gifts of God come only when you become His teammate in manifesting the truth. Then the partnership blossoms. Then the truth within you pours forth into the lifetime experience that you want beyond any priceless gem. The experience on the earth plane brings you the greatest satisfaction possible with God as Partner. This is the key message of this book.

"When the true union takes place between you and God, goals, tenderness, and greatness manifest into the perfect alliance with what the nature of God IS. Then you may realize your best dreams, your hidden goals, perfect relationships, the perfection of your body, and the development of your true personality which reflects the nature of God. These and more will belong to you who advance into union with God."

Now and then people say to me, "I guess a person must be really wonderful to be able to get God-mind truth." I asked the Brotherhood how to answer that statement.

"Teamwork is the key—not the person who is already perfect. The way to receive the gifts of God is to open your mind, not enter into a closet of old thoughts and concepts. The key to perfect demonstration is to align yourself with the very nature of God. That way you become His partner, His perfect thought-form.

"The thought-form—you—then enters into teamwork with this great God. The wonderful gifts He has to give then become yours to use. There is no purpose in entering some monastic existence in order to deserve God. Nor is there any good accomplished by entering into the 'holier than thou' syndrome in order to be seen by people as one who is 'better' than others. This sort of thing repels the God nature because it enters into a limited concept. Remember, a limited God concept limits your demonstration.

"And if you think God only selects a few to give His gifts to, you're very wrong. God enters to give, not to take. Giving is His nature. The God of the Universe eternalizes what is most wonderful, not what is inferior. Therefore, only by your acceptance of His partnership, His wonderful gifts, His participation in the teamwork to make your life what you want it to be can these things we tell you of come about.

"The tender truth enters the mind, and it says, 'Team up with me, the truth that enters you from God-mind.' Your heart responds to it, right? The gentle truth is ready to become one with you who will then enter it into manifestation. Making truth one with your inner being, however much time it takes, is needed if you will make the demonstration in the market-place of your life. This truth reaches out with its best eternalizations, but if you neglect this step of becoming one with the truth, no amount of trust in the Partner, God, will make the truth enter into demonstration.

"You may ask, 'Why?' Because God only does what God does. He opens Himself and all that He IS to you, but He never takes over your spirit self, for you may accept or refuse what God IS. Give this message your understanding, your complete union, your powerful thought. Then act.

"Team up with what the entity who is writing this book says to you. Her own story of how she opened her mind, opened her heart and eventually learned to act upon the truth will enter in the next chapter to give you the story of one person's teaming up with the Brotherhood. Then, as she advances in her understanding of what happens in our relationship, perhaps you, the reader, will better relate to what this book is about.

"Present the truth to your truth center. Then align yourself with it in the temple which eternalizes the best of your hopes, dreams and desires. This teamwork places the truth there for you. What you do with it is up to you. But no one is expected to work all alone. That is why we enter the scene now, to tell you that it is time to make this team of you, this Brotherhood and God work in the living of your life.

"We near the end of our transmissions to this writer in the book, 'Eternal Gold.' The truth of her being and the truth of your being, dear reader, is in the hands of each of you, but remember, teamwork is the key to success.

"Never tell yourself that this is all imagination! Entering into a self-deluding concept only leads to defeat. The open channel is real, all right. This channel, that we help you build until you can do this on your own, is your way to reach through the earth-mind barrier to the source of truth—God-mind.

"Now enter into the gentle truth; be the one to understand and to act."

CHAPTER 19

THE OPENING OF A MIND

The Brotherhood of God has asked me to write my own story of how I began this communication with them. "Tell how resistant you were then, how hesitant, how everlasting full of questions you were," they said. "Then when the truth progressed into you, tell them how your mind opened little by little and our communication grew."

A good friend recently noted several changes in me. She said the Jean Foster she used to know was not as insistent on her own identity as this Jean Foster. "I was startled to hear you vehemently insist on using your own first name instead of using the married version—Mrs. Carl Foster. You had always avoided controversy, and I could hardly believe my ears to hear you making several bold and definite statements about your individuality.

"And another thing," she added, "I told you long ago that I had a personal library of metaphysical books, channeled writing, and various other interesting books that you could borrow. But you never seemed interested until the past few years."

How could that be? I've always been interested in such things!

But how long ago does the word "always" apply to my life?

Let's start at the beginning of my story, or what I perceive to be the beginning. Awareness of another dimension to my life began probably three or four years before this writing. Dreams crowded my sleep, and I wrote them down and sought interpretation based on some recommended studies. Often I woke up at night feeling that I was surrounded with people, and I would ask aloud, "Who are all those people?"

Full sentences stayed clearly in my mind when I woke in the night, words full of spiritual awareness. But their meaning for my life eluded me. What was trying to come through? Why were these messages flooding my sleep?

The rest of my life was on an even keel after a couple of difficult years. The roller coaster emotions and physical unevenness had disappeared. Good nutrition and exercise solved a diabetes problem. A new interest in playing the recorder—an instrument whose heyday was in the 14th and 15th centuries—challenged me and brought me into contact with a group of interesting musicians. My relationship with my husband changed, but for the better, I think. I became more emotionally independent, and I began to live my life alongside him rather than through him. I had even managed to free myself emotionally from our three grown children, and in doing so I freed them.

Part of me viewed these changes rather like an observer who stays interested but uninvolved. This observer in me pointed out areas that needed changing, and the other me did the work involved. For example, the observer in me pointed out, "You are much too sensitive to your husband's every word and action." Thereupon, I withdrew my constant tuning in to his life. No, it wasn't easy. In fact, it hurt because I had insisted we share everything in our lives. I suppose the sharing was some sort of romantic ideal, but it wasn't conducive to our individual development. Though it may seem strange, I never questioned the need for the changes. The observer and I formed a subtle partnership while we stabilized the life of the one called Jean K. Foster.

During this same time period, I read books about the possibility of communication with an advanced spirit in the next plane of life. Guides, advisers, whatever they might be, I knew I wanted that experience in my life. No, I was not afraid. I had a feeling of recognition about such a communication, a feeling of warmth, of anticipation, of real joy.

October 14, 1984, I began an experiment in automatic writing. It was three months before I was in contact with the Brotherhood of God. Each day I tried to feel the presence of God around me before I offered my pencil to whomever. I didn't do this out of fear, however. There was no hypnosis or trance; I was very wide awake and in charge. When the writing finally began, it consisted of swirls that resembled my second grade efforts at mastering cursive writing. I put questions at the top of a sheet of plain paper. "Why should I continue automatic writing? Who is writing through me?" Again came the never ending practice session of m's and l's with an occasional readable word.

In spite of what I considered poor progress, I persisted in this daily appointment until fragmentary messages began to appear. "More people plan——" followed by a practice session on p's and u's. The first sentence that made sense went like this: "Tell yourself that you will be just a traveler in this place."

Not realizing that I must ask for a teacher in order to get one, I quietly waited for someone, anyone, to "take my pencil." The messages that soon began in earnest came from spirits who had something to say to someone still in the earth life. A few of these messages were repeated over and over.

Not knowing what to do with these communications, and having *no* interest in becoming a medium, I asked for a teacher. I wrote these words on my paper: *"Could I Please have a teacher?"* Thereupon, my fingers were impelled, so it seemed to me, to write the word "Love." This word, I soon learned, represented the presence of my requested teacher, a kind, helpful spirit who readied me for the greatest experience of my life.

I continued my daily appointment but told no one else what I was doing. Questions were directed to my teacher, and as answers came, often the key word or words did not come through. Frustrated, I stared at the writing, alternating between feelings of complete defeat and angry determination. Was it worth it? What was to be accomplished here?

Love met me each day by signing in, and again we'd work to communicate. To create a quiet, centered mind, I focused on a place on the east Florida coast where I had been happy, carefree, and united with all that flew, swam or crawled. I recreated details of that scene in detail, from the foul smell of sulphur water bubbling from a pipe in a shallow well to the slightest fishy odor of the salt air from the ocean. Mentally, I stood again on the high bank overlooking the green Atlantic, and I followed the familiar path to the weathered wooden steps leading down to the soft, often hot sand.

Again I walked in the cool foam of the surf that broke on the shore. I watched the multicolored periwinkles burrow down into the sand after each wave uncovered them. I listened to the white gulls calling sharply to one another while they end-lessly examined the shoreline, wings extended, gliding in the wind. The brown feathered pelicans, sometimes alone, some-times in the company of one or two others, flapped their wings gracefully as they passed. One caught the wind just right and the flapping ceased. Lower and lower it drifted—a hunter whose awkward shape belied its ability to dive straight down into the water for its target. It momentarily disappeared and then re-surfaced with its pouch distended.

When the heat of the sun warmed me, I was ready for Love to write through my hand. Question: "Do you have any sugges-tions for the living of my life to promote a growth of conscious-ness?"

"Clear your primer of most life memories and make today . . . Clear your . . . of useless memories and make other memories. Close out old hurts. Love will only make your mem-ories clear away old hurts and clean away the life. More will come to you as you love more." The dots, of course, represent the words that I did not get. However, I had cleared a big hur-dle, for I had a clear statement in answer to a question.

In December of that same year, about two weeks before Christmas, Love asked me to go to my typewriter and position my fingers on the keys. The following material is part of what I received: "Now. I must open your heart. Open your heart. Open your heart. I open my heart, open my heart to you. No one iwm (sic) open open open open open . . . "

Exasperation stirred inside me. Would this spirit never stop with this open-your-eyes business?

"Zombie! Open your eyes!"

I opened my eyes, all right—with a start! That part of the transmission poured out in a torrent, and my fingers worked fast to keep up.

Then the communication continued. "I must open your

heart, open your heart."

"To what?" I typed.

"Open your heart, open your heart, maybe open your, open your heart."

Annoyed, I typed, "Can we progress to another point?" However, the same words went on and on and on until a new word crept into the transmission.

"Open your immortal open, immortal soul to immortality. Open your soul to immortality."

At this point I tired of trying to get some sense into the material and asked if this was enough for one day. "I team up in union on union. I now open your open, open mind. I team up with you—union. Love. Goodbye."

Day after day I spent from thirty minutes to an hour practicing the reception from Love. One day shortly after the above transmission, I decided on a more conversational approach. It started with Love's usual message. "I open your heart. I open your mind to the heart of God."

"Wonderful," I both thought and typed.

"I open your heart, open your mind to good."

"How can I help accomplish this?" I asked, and then inspired, I made a statement of my belief. "I believe in Love as a presence, I believe in immortality, and I believe in a great goodness called God."

Love responded, "Please do not open your eyes to promises of omniscient God believing in your imprudent insight."

Humbled, I concentrated on receiving instead of giving my own self-important thoughts. One morning about 10 a.m., Love greeted me in this way: "I think you take too much time to be ready. I want you to begin by taking the important things on opening your eyes."

Stung by what I called criticism, I argued, "I have responsibilities first thing in the morning."

Love responded, "I only mean that you open your eyes planning the time."

Petulantly I asked, "Can we begin now?"

"I have time now. Money isn't only important on your plot of earth. It is important here."

Still smarting from what I took as a reprimand, I typed, "We can't take it with us, can we?"

"I think you only jest," Love responded. "I am serious. I want you to understand the spiritual equivalent of money." He had my attention. "I open your eyes to this now. This is the truth. I want you to open your eyes. I eventually want you to open your mind too." Again the sardonic tone. I gritted my teeth. "I open your heart to the truth. I give no promises over the phone. I give promises in person. I think you need to open your mind to the truth of the spirit. I want important things to penetrate to the portion of your brain that gives out information."

Our conversation continued with Love continually urging me to open my mind. This spirit also told me, "I think you plot on the phone too much. I only need you one hour." Give up my telephone conversations? This spirit was certainly asking a lot of me.

My questions poured out. Love answered them. We discussed psychic books. We analyzed my use of time, my relationships with friends, energy spent on my dogs, my role as wife, and above all, the development of our communication which was to culminate in the writing of a "tome."

January 1, 1985, almost four months into this communication, Love began by saying, "I have only the time/space project to talk about." That was the name given to our communication. "Give your open mind to the tome (one of several books on the same subject). Every time you write on this project you will be happy. Tell the world that you get this material through the open channel of the Brotherhood."

I talked about the articles I wrote and the juvenile mystery I had completed but not sold. I said that the worst problem I had was marketing the material. There was a slight pause, and then, "The biggest problem you have is procrastination."

Over and over the truth that I tried to hide, even from myself, was brought into the open. Again and again the communicator penetrated past my rationalizations. I was an open book to Love and to this (thus far) mysterious Brotherhood. They read my thoughts. They knew my subterfuge and ferreted it into the light. I had to face myself as I really was, not as I hoped others would see me or as I wanted to be.

January 2, 1985, I received my assignment from a new spirit. "I thought you would never get ready. This is the most important work you have to do." Love had not signed in. Who was giving me this message?

"I need your plotting now," the messenger continued.

"This is still morning." My tone, whether the spirit knew it or not was cold and questioning.

"I plot in the very early morning," came the answer.

"Why do you say 'plot'?" I typed. "That word indicates a devious plan."

"Plotting is the name of the important pieces of our operation. Plot is the word that will be used."

I hesitated a moment, and then typed on my paper, "You seem very dictatorial."

"I am only being open with you." No hesitation at all with this answer.

"And I with you." I tried to be equally straightforward.

"I only want your hour—each ounce of it."

"Am I talking to Love?" I typed.

"No. This is your operator. I operate your mind."

Operator indeed! "No! Love said that I was not to be dictated to. I have free will."

"I only want one hour to be trusted," came the message.

"I want to talk to Love!" I was determined and firm.

"I only want one hour."

"If Love says OK, then I am willing." There was the slightest of hesitations as if they might have exchanged shrugs and sighs, and then Love responded. How did I know it was Love? The feel of the being, the personality that I had come to know, made itself known to me. Not a very definite or concrete answer, but I can only compare it to the feeling I have when I am with various people. There is just "that feeling" about each one that I identify with.

"Love." There was the sign-in that I expected. "This is Love. I open your eyes to love. I see you are doubting that I may open your eyes to plot."

"Is Love in charge of this project or not?" I asked.

"I only want that you begin to write. Only begin to write."

I did. As long as I was in charge, what could happen? So the Brotherhood of God and I got acquainted through counseling, and our communication began to flow in eloquence, at least on their part. I learned that Love is a specialist who helps people like me who want to make contact with God-mind by writing what they receive. He is a trainer.

Words like "plot" disappeared from the transmission, and as I turned myself fully toward the enlightenment that came daily, the vocabulary became more extensive and beautiful. Archaic words like "pontification" soon disappeared too. The only thing that did not change completely was this writer. I still held out against certain thoughts and concepts.

I capitulated to the urgency of getting to my typewriter early in the morning. Friends, when they heard I was writing in the mornings, desisted from calling. The pattern for my use of time was finally established just as Love wanted it to be in the first place.

"The tome needs your best efforts to understand. Use this channel to be the best interpreter of the open mind channel. This is the truth of growth—that we have an open channel between us, plane I and plane II.

"You grow in truth by opening your mind to this plane. You open your mind to us and tell others that by doing this you will be more spiritual." Again, I frowned and hesitated, but the message continued. "You need to be the channel of growth in this Brotherhood. You will be a bonafide worker. Be patient with this Brotherhood; be patient with the growth. Believe in this work, and I will bring you the best of the growth. Be sure that this is the best part of your day on this, our tome."

I was evidently approved and "hired" to be the writer of the Brotherhood's books. And along with my acceptance of this assignment came new energy that flowed steadily day by day. Most of my resistance to what I received faded, for the beauty and truth of the words were irresistible.

From this point on I began to receive material that later I organized into the first seven chapters of "The God-mind Connection." The other seven chapters were organized by the Brotherhood, and we worked, chapter by chapter to the end. I was directed to make the language modern and in good form. Whenever I made a change, I asked the Brotherhood to give me an opinion on it. Sometimes it was "OK." Other times it lacked something I was to put in. They urged me to incorporate my questions into the material that they might give enlightenment not only to me, but to the reader.

Even at this point I did not accept all that was given. I often stopped, reread the material, frowned at the words, even rejected what was given. The Brotherhood, however, persisted with explanations, and they never backed down on any point they gave.

Finally, we came to a chapter that gave information that I found difficult to accept. The material concerned me. They told me this hard-to-believe story to help me, they said, to understand the importance of the writing I was doing. And what's even harder, they expected me to share this with the readers.

Here it is in a capsulized form: I am the second spirit to inhabit my body. Yes, they explained that when Jean K. Foster had been deeply depressed and ill, she wanted to leave her body. Memories flooded back. I remembered several times saying, "I don't have a tight grip on life." I wanted to let go. My purpose in life seemed over, I had found no new purpose, I didn't feel well, and I was afraid I was becoming a poor mate for my husband whom I loved very much.

No one, the Brotherhood assured me, is simply "taken over" by a second spirit. Apparently, when the body slept, the spirit self of my body discussed the matter with the one who was to replace it. "One day when you were napping, the change took place." They say giving up our bodies to another spirit is like giving a total body transplant to an advanced spirit who comes with some special purpose in mind. They also say that my subconscious knows there have been two spirits, and they pointed out certain dreams I had which should have told me this.

The second spirit always comes to bring order to the earth life. That is the first assignment. The responsibilities and affections of the first spirit also become the responsibilities and affections of the second. After the life becomes harmonious, the second occupant may go about accomplishing his plan. My plan, apparently, was to write these books.

"The God-mind Connection" was completed by late April or early May, 1985. The title of the second book, "The Truth That Goes Unclaimed," was presented to me by the Brotherhood along with the titles of twenty chapters one morning in May. From then on I worked daily to receive the material for these chapters which my husband and I then edited into as readable a form as possible without changing the unique style and the great beauty of their own thought expression.

This book, "Eternal Gold," was presented in the same way as "The Truth that Goes Unclaimed." However, in this book the Brotherhood assigned me the task of writing Chapter 19 all by myself. It has not been easy, nor has it been a fast piece of writing. In fact, it has taken me more than twice the time to write this chapter as it did to take down one of the Brotherhood's chapters and to edit it, too.

If I say at this point that most of my questioning is over, I am sure to receive a new challenge of some kind that will prove me wrong. Most of my own spirit work shows up in the books I write because the Brotherhood insists that I work through all the truth that they bring to the books. If I don't work with the truth, how can I be honest? At least the Brotherhood sees it this way.

I am having a great spiritual adventure, one that I came to this earth life to have. I did not come to my body as one who had advanced beyond the need of help, you understand. I came with two purposes in mind, according to the Brotherhood. I came to write these truth books, and I came to become one with as much truth as I can. Former lifetimes reveal the need for much work on my part while in this present experience. Therefore, I work as you do to put truth foremost in my thinking. I want to shed the earth-mind truth, and I want to link myself with God-mind truth that pours through the open channel shown me by the Brotherhood of God.

Note from the Brotherhood:

"The truth that this chapter reveals will help you be the perfect thought projection of the God-mind truth. This writer knows that she is spirit, not body. Enter into this thought that the only reality is spirit, and you will then have the perspective to work with the God-mind truth to produce a perfect experience in your lifetime.

"Team up with the Brotherhood to enter into the wonderful truth that is there for you, the truth that will enter into the greatest adventure you will ever know."